"*Koreaworld* offers so much more than recipes. This book is a whirlwind introduction to a whole [...] entirely new perspective on Korean [...] everything, go to Seoul, and eat at all [...] fun!" —Ruth Reichl, journalist and author of *The Paris Novel*

"I love the way Matt writes—this is an incredibly inspirational look into the world of Korean food." —Jamie Oliver, chef and author of *5 Ingredients Mediterranean*

"*Koreaworld* is more than a cookbook; it traces the remarkable journey of modern Korean cuisine from its roots in Korea's bustling cities to its vibrant evolution in the United States, creating a bridge that spans continents and time, uniting the rich heritage and a culture." —Eunjo Park, former executive chef of Momofuku Kāwi

"The wide range of modern Korean food is on display in this fascinating book that is as electric, sumptuous, and diverse as the cuisine it portrays." —Edward Lee, chef and author of *Bourbon Land*

"If you've ever wanted to feel like a local, use *Koreaworld* as your guide. Deuki and Matt have curated something that pushes well past the utility of recipes. This is a showcase of Korean culture, as it exists. More so, it continues the conversation of what it means to be Korean today." —Daniel Harthausen, winner of HBO's *Big Brunch* and chef-owner of Young Mother

KOREAWORLD: A COOKBOOK
코리아 월드

Deuki Hong & Matt Rodbard
Photographs by Alex Lau

Clarkson Potter/Publishers
New York

CONTENTS

INTRODUCTION

AND

SOME

QUESTIONS

AND

ANSWERS

**You are
about to read
the story
of a culinary
revolution.**

Korean food is exploding around the world, found in the homes, restaurants, hearts, and stewpots of people from Seoul and Los Angeles to New York City, Shanghai, Portland, Paris, and beyond. Korean food and culture are at the epicenter of innovation, not just in the United States and Korea but around the world. It can feel like the Korean Wave (dubbed Hallyu) touches nearly everybody and anybody consuming food, music, literature, and Netflix melodramas. It's a story that needed telling, and in a big way.

In this book, we capture the modern excitement around Korean food through stories of chefs and home cooks and the exciting recipes that are shaping the modern Korean kitchen, from centuries-old traditions to next-wave dishes that feel like they were invented overnight. (And we means Deuki and Matt and our photographer buddy, Alex.)

While Korean food knows no borders—we've personally cooked in a modern Korean restaurant in Iceland—this is a book that focuses on two primary areas we know best: modern Korea itself and Koreatowns and Korean-inspired kitchens throughout the United States.

During our over two years of travels specifically for this book—and a decade of exploration prior—we met hundreds of restaurant owners, farmers, shopkeepers, a few Buddhist monks, a couple of massively popular YouTubers, a professional golfer, and many others who hold Korean food and culture at the center of their lives. Among our visits to Korea were trips in the fall of 2021 and 2022, spending time in a country that was facing many of the global trials of a post-pandemic world and oftentimes emerging with exceedingly fresh ideas and innovation. And back here in the United States, we've talked with Korean immigrants, the children of Korean immigrants, Korean adoptees, and others who are simply inspired by all aspects of Korean cuisine and culture.

In this book, we've collected the stories and recipes from these Citizens of Koreaworld (we count ourselves and our recipes among them), and through all of these conversations, we've seen many different perspectives on what "modern" Korean food is—dishes that reach back, dishes that look forward, dishes that represent a personal point of view, and dishes that seem timeless and universal. These include (and these are only a few) tteokbokki turned rose with cream, fried chicken showered with crispy anchovies and shishito peppers, and giant beef short ribs smoked in hay and then grilled (and a radish kimchi granita to serve with them). We travel to Jeolla-do and taste the best vegan broccoli salad topped with a spicy, salty ssamjang mayo (Vegenaise, of course), and when we get to Jeju Island, we experience a whole fried (and smashed) gochujang-seasoned fish that has changed the way we cook fish at home. Back in the United States, we fry rice with pineapple kimchi and add kimchi to pimento cheese in a chapter tackling the big, bold, sometimes controversial world of fusion cooking. And we cover sweets and snacks—hello, banana milk cake. As some of you may know, Koreans are masters of the snack and bring recipes for popcorn dusted with kimchi salt and an inventive way to soup up that package of Shin Ramyun.

Expanding beyond recipes, we touch on the modern history of Korea and the Korean diaspora through short essays and visits to some places less covered in the Western media. We're excited to show you our journey around Koreaworld. But how did we get here exactly? Let's go back a bit. Starting in 2012, we spent over two years traveling to the Koreatowns of the United States (especially in Los Angeles, Atlanta, and New York) to research our first cookbook, *Koreatown,* interviewing more than one hundred chefs and business owners.

Once back in our New York City kitchens, we developed recipes that reflected traditional home and restaurant cooking. We made an emphatic call for readers to look beyond grilled meat (widely known as "Korean barbecue") and fusion cooking like kimchi tacos to embrace the more traditional dishes that have been beloved—and cooked ubiquitously—in Koreatowns for generations. Gamjatang (pork neck and perilla seed stew), yukgaejang (fiery shredded beef soup), and yukhwe (raw rib eye seasoned with sesame oil and orchard fruit and served chilled) received equivalent real estate alongside such well-known favorites as kalbi (marinated short ribs) and twice-fried chicken.

Since its publication in 2016, *Koreatown* has continued to be read and cooked from (thank you, friends on Instagram, for sharing all those kimchi bokkeumbap photos). But within a few years of finishing it, we started talking about what changes we were seeing in Korean food. Our conversations, between busy jobs while living on opposite coasts, weren't first focused on writing another book. They were more about our shared observations of how exciting and inspiring the Korean food scene—and Korean culture as a whole—had become, not just in the United States but also in Korea. As we started to talk, we realized that the simultaneous evolution and spread of Korean food and culture was one of the biggest cultural stories in the world, period. We needed to get to work, and the result is this book you hold. Welcome to *Koreaworld*.

When people find out that we are writing a book about modern Korean food, the reaction is often one of great interest and excitement quickly followed by questions. Here are a few of the most frequently asked ones. They not only cover topics we've encountered during our many travels while working on this book but also go back well before that too.

When *did* Korean food get huge in the United States?

This is an interesting question. It would be wildly inaccurate to say that Korean food didn't have a clear slot in American food culture when we were writing our first book. Korean immigration is one of America's success stories. After the passage of the Immigration and Nationality Act of 1965, which removed quotas that strongly favored European immigration, the Korean immigrant population in the United States boomed, rising from 11,000 in 1960 to 290,000 in 1980. The Korean-born population grew to 568,000 in 2000 and peaked at 1.1 million immigrants in 2010—slightly ticking down to 1,039,000 in 2019, according to the US Census.

It's important to contextualize Korean immigration to understand what came next. When we started writing our first book in the summer of 2013, Korean restaurants, like Korean-owned dry cleaners and bodegas, were woven into not just Korean American society but urban culture as a whole, particularly in communities like Los Angeles, New York City, and the outskirts of Atlanta and Washington, DC. But the deep bench of braises, stews, grilled meats, and seasoned vegetables that we have all grown to love were rarely name-checked in established media outlets. Kimchi was known and starting to find its way into non-Korean refrigerators, and thanks in part to Roy Choi's culinary and social media skills, Mexican and Korean cuisines had merged at the launch of the popular Kogi Korean BBQ taco truck in November 2008. But both fundamental and trending Korean cooking concepts like banchan (the meal's introductory small plates), jorim (seasoned and simmered foods), kimjang (kimchi-making season), plant-based temple cuisine, dalgona coffee, and ssam (outside of Momofuku's famed slow-roasted whole pork shoulder Bo Ssäm, which in the end wasn't actually ssam) were hardly part of mainstream conversations.

Catching us up to the current times, what recipes and stories did you know you needed to include in *Koreaworld*?

Of course, there were so many recipes to consider. And the number of inspiring chefs and Korean food professionals with unique stories to tell is staggering. We had our work cut out for us. In *Koreatown,* our goal was to survey some of the amazing dishes we found in Koreatowns around the United States, from kimchi, namul (seasoned vegetables), and various banchan to the greatest hits of jjigaes (stews) and tangs (soups). In *Koreaworld,* we are filling in some of the gaps we missed the first time around and, more important, really digging into what Koreans in Korea are excited about today and what the Citizens of Koreaworld are inspired by in their Korean American lives. Our many trips to Korea and around the United States have informed this book deeply, and on a number of occasions we shared a meal—or dined solo—in Seoul or San Francisco or Portland, Oregon, or Gwangju or Washington, DC, and made a mental (or physical) note to take some piece of knowledge back to the kitchen. But by no means are we considering this an encyclopedia. Maangchi, we're looking at you for that one!

We knew we needed to cover kimbap (page 211), the beloved rice rolls made famous in part through the popular K-drama *Extraordinary Attorney Woo* and the inventiveness of the incredibly talented chef Eunjo Park (see page 208). There's a thirty-minute version of jokbal (page 159), the popular anju of spiced and braised pigs' trotters, and honey butter corn ribs (page 201) inspired by the popular chips.

We knew it was time to update our doenjang jjigae recipe (page 41), which Deuki has changed every couple of years since he's been cooking professionally. We felt like our pancake output could be upped a bit, and meals at Kanggane Maetdol Bindaetteok in Seoul's Hannam neighborhood and at Queens in San Francisco confirmed our need to dive deeper into the world of jeon (pages 53 and 55). Inspired by a slight cultural shift away from alcohol for nights out in both Korea and the United States, we wanted to tackle nonalcoholic drinks.

When he's not writing this cookbook or running restaurants, Deuki runs a bakery and ice cream shop, and along with his partner, Elaine Lau, we wanted to expand the way we think about Korean-inspired desserts, including a vanilla chiffon cake that draws on the flavors of convenience-store banana milks (banana mat uyu, page 265). The recipes we've chosen to include here tap into both Korean traditions and the fresh new ways Korean food is being interpreted around the world. Picking the recipes to feature was the biggest challenge, but they're also the book's greatest strength.

Have *Squid Game, Parasite,* and the meteoric rise of K-pop fandom in the United States changed the way Korean food is viewed?

This is something we've thought about for some time! A part of us would like to think that the scenes featuring the honeycomb-like dalgona candy (page 271) in the 2021 dystopian survival thriller *Squid Game* have gotten the masses thinking more about Korea's singular foods. This is not to mention the kimchi slap heard around the internet from a 2014 episode of the drama *Everybody Say Kimchi.* After the clip went viral, we imagine that the Seamless orders for kimchi jjigae went nuts in certain parts of the country.

In Euny Hong's wonderful book, *The Birth of Korean Cool: How One Nation Is Conquering the World through Pop Culture,* the journalist examines the concept of Hallyu, which can be summarized as the focused effort (that is, investment) by the South Korean government to export Korean dramas, gaming, and music first to China and eventually around the world. Food gets swept up in this wave, too, and we've each been hired at various times by Korean governmental organizations to help promote Korean food in the United States. The bureaucratic approach to Korean food promotion has admittedly been met with mixed results, and we'd like to think that the inherent beauty and deliciousness of the food are enough to sell it. But you can't deny the power of a global TV hit on Netflix and the legion of BTS fans thinking a little bit more deeply about Korean food.

Who shot these incredible photos?! And how did you decide to approach photography this way?

Alex Lau! We've long been fans of Alex's work, and it was during our two-plus years of reporting and eating and shooting that we formed a real friendship with our guy (and favorite nationally ranked powerlifter). The photos in this book bring the "world" in *Koreaworld* to life—and we shot every frame in the field, intentionally avoiding the traditional studio food shoot. All the food in this book was shot at the source, cooked honestly, and served on real plates with real utensils and on real surfaces.

With this approach, some of the recipes appear with photos that illustrate the spirit of the dish—not an exactly plated replica but rather a moment in the field that inspired our final recipe (though you will know you did it "right" if your final dish ends up looking like the photo). We also shot many of the recipes with the creator of the dish at our side, which was thrilling for us and allowed us to style the food exactly how the originator wanted it done. We think this documentary approach makes for a stronger read, and we hope you enjoy joining us on the journey.

01

MODERN KOREA

Let's begin with a deep look at the foods of both urban and rural Korea, with stories and recipes illustrating how the cooking within the country's borders continues to inspire the world many times over. Yet Korea's current status isn't only because of the food. In 2018, the Winter Olympics were held in Pyeonchang, cementing Korea's place on the world's stage. This was also when Deuki visited Korea for the first time since his birth (he appeared on NBC's *Today* show during the coverage of the games). The trip was a life-changing event, reuniting him with family and providing him with an opportunity to explore Korea and forge new friendships that remain strong today.

This section covers many of the dishes Koreans in Korea are eating today and how many of these recipes, ingredients, techniques, and general cooking philosophies may be hitting the United States sooner than you think. The early part explores the bustling urban metropolis of Seoul with its nearly ten million residents. In it we break down some of the big ideas we spotted on the streets and in the restaurants during our numerous visits since publishing *Koreatown*.

Then we hit the country and coasts to explore another side of Korea. Jeolla-do is often considered Korea's breadbasket, and the rural province two hundred miles south of Seoul is where we spent time learning about temple cuisine through the eyes of a workaday chef tasked with feeding a hundred hungry monks daily. Jeong Kwan is the Buddhist chef who rose to fame through a memorable 2017 *Chef's Table* episode that brought attention to the region, but we found out that there's even more going on in the temples than what is shown on Netflix.

The mystical, subtropical, tourist-centric, and thus Hawaii-esque Jeju Island covers over seven hundred square miles, and we visited to taste heukdwaeji (black pig barbecue) and to explore the island's unique microclimates and craft brewing. We encountered incredible seafood and dove into the legend of the haenyeo.

In a shorter chapter, we relate tales of our time in Gangwon-do to taste bibim guksu (buckwheat crepes) and hike around Seoraksan National Park, one of Korea's most strikingly beautiful places to visit.

Korea is certainly no monolith, and it's impossible to define the spirit of modern Korea in a sentence or a page. But what we did find were surprises around every corner—and cooking with the core ingredients—jang (soybean paste), dubu (bean curd), kim (seaweed), bap (rice)—in ways we couldn't even imagine back in New York and San Francisco. There have been new developments in coffee, with Seoul alone welcoming more than one thousand shops opening in recent years, bringing the grand total to more than fifteen thousand. We found a thriving modern café culture that takes hints from Europe and America but with a fresh Korean spark. And Korean barbecue is on another level. This is all to say, we soaked it all up, along with the short rib smoke and new adventures in ssamjang, and have put the highlights on the pages of this section.

We begin our journey in Seoul, the country's urban capital that geographically unifies majestic mountains and urban sprawl; a maze of quiet alleys, with a single kimbap stand at the end; and sardine can–like intersections where it feels like the population of nearly ten million is packed onto a single avenue. We tell this story of Seoul broadly with recipes and ideas that we spotted throughout the city: a "roasted" version of samgyetang (chicken and ginseng soup), a near-surgical construction of jeon (pancakes), and the incredibly expressive espresso and baking scene that has recently taken over the country.

Next, we focus on how Korean barbecue is being prepared in Seoul in ways that push the sizzling grill into exciting new territory. Since the KBBQ standards are well covered elsewhere (including in *Koreatown*), we feature instead a giant short rib lightly smoked with hay and new adventures with banchan—namely 7UP pickles and a kkakdugi (cubed radish kimchi) granita. And there's a method for post-barbecue bokkeumbap (fried rice) that we think needs to end every at-home KBBQ session.

During our travels to the city in the fall of 2021 and 2022, we connected with some of the key figures shaping the city's culinary movement— individuals looking back at the country's long and rich history while pushing the cuisine fully forward. We sat down with Mingoo Kang, one of Korea's modern chef heroes, to find out the story behind Mingles, his Michelin-starred restaurant in Seoul, and to cook through some of his favorite recipes, including a bowl of brothy anchovy noodles.

Rapid transformation of urban life (some may call it gentrification) has its victims, of course, and Jason Kim, a Korean American who moved to Seoul and writes the intoxicating blog and Instagram account My Korean Eats, helped bring attention to one of Seoul's greatest (and dying) neighborhoods, Euljiro, while offering a proper eulogy for the closing businesses. But looking forward, we also got to visit with Seoul-based YouTube star Tina Choi and asked about her journey from shy and bookish lab assistant to one of Korean food's biggest global ambassadors, with millions of subscribers on the platform. Her recipe for a unique egg dish inspired by spicy tofu stew—and by the Middle East— serves as a view to just one way the culture is evolving. It is but a single adventure of the many we write about in this journey through Seoul.

ROSE TTEOKBOKKI
SAUTÉED RICE CAKES WITH GOCHUJANG AND CREAM
로제 떡볶이

SERVES 4

We wanted to step back for a second and think about the transformation of tteokbokki over the past decade. While so much of Korean cooking got spicier and more extreme, the classic, all-day utility dish made of rice cakes, fish cakes, and fiery gochujang went . . . pink. Enter rose tteokbokki, a gentle, creamy version that has grown in popularity in Korea. Begin with frozen rice cakes. They're better for this dish than fresh ones, which tend to break down easily and lose their shape. The key to adding flavor to the rice cakes is to simmer them gently in a light bath of salt and sugar in advance. Deuki spotted this technique at a market in Seoul and hasn't looked back.

Another twist here is the addition of apple preserves or syrup. Layering in subtle sweetness is a good way to counter the heat of the chile paste. Some home cooks like to add ketchup, but the preference here is for apple, a more natural form of sweetness. The final step is the addition of cream, which gives the dish its namesake hue. Use as much or as little as you want, or skip the step fully if fire-engine red is your favorite shade for sautéed rice cakes.

3 cups cylinder-shaped rice cakes (garaeddeok)

1 tablespoon kosher salt

5 tablespoons sugar

6½ cups water

¼ cup neutral cooking oil

¼ cup thinly sliced scallions, white and green parts, plus more for garnish

6 garlic cloves, minced

¼ cup gochujang

¼ cup diced fish cake

¼ cup diced bacon or hot dog

¼ cup shredded green cabbage

2 tablespoons apple preserves or fruit syrup, homemade (page 149) or store-bought

1 tablespoon soy sauce

1 teaspoon MSG (optional)

½ cup heavy cream, or as needed

2 tablespoons sesame seeds, for garnish

1   In a medium saucepan, combine the rice cakes, salt, 3 tablespoons of the sugar, and 4 cups of the water and bring to a gentle simmer over medium heat. Cook for about 20 minutes. Do not boil! This step adds flavor and improves the texture of the rice cakes. Drain the rice cakes and set aside.

2   In a large skillet or wok, heat the oil over low heat. Add the scallions and garlic and cook, stirring often, until fragrant, about 5 minutes. This allows the flavors of the scallions and garlic to marry with the oil, providing a more aromatic flavor base.

3   Add the gochujang and cook, stirring often, for 2 to 3 minutes more. This step cooks off the strong gochujang flavor and extracts its oils for additional spice.

4   Add the reserved rice cakes, the fish cake, bacon, and cabbage, stir together well, and then fry in the fat, stirring occasionally, until light golden brown and caramelized, 2 to 3 minutes.

5   Add the remaining 2½ cups water and 2 tablespoons sugar, the apple preserves, soy sauce, and MSG (if using), stir well, and simmer for 2 minutes to dissolve the sugar and blend the flavors.

6   With the heat still on low, gradually add the cream, stopping when you achieve the shade of rose you desire. Serve immediately, garnished with sesame seeds and scallions.

SAMGYETANG TONGDAK
RICE AND GINSENG–STUFFED ROAST CHICKEN
삼계탕 통닭

SERVES 3 OR 4

At Hannamdong Hanbang Tongdak, the clipboard starts to fill up with names an hour before the 5:00 p.m. opening, as hungry diners linger around one of the most impressive restaurant setups in all of Seoul. Thirty chickens, each stuffed with the ingredients of the fortifying and herbaceous samgyetang (chicken stuffed with glutinous rice, ginseng, and jujubes, then cooked and served in soup), are neatly lined up on a spit, roasting and rotating in various states of golden brown as a wood fire roars beneath. Samgyetang is one of Korea's foundational soups (tang), and on a fall visit to the city's Hannam-dong neighborhood, we stopped in our tracks at this sight and were able to snag an early seat. Samgyetang roasted chicken? Yes, please.

This is our own version of the Hannamdong Hanbang Tongdak dish, and we've included a few time-saving steps that may suit you. The easiest way to gather the ginseng and jujubes you'll need is to seek out a samgyetang kit at your local H Mart or Asian supermarket. The sweet and fiery dipping sauce is not required, but it's the sauce that we most associate with Korean-style roasted chicken. For fans of chicken and rice, this is a creative spin we think is great for a weeknight dinner or a showstopping weekend dinner-party set piece — with the grand reveal being the carving of the bird tableside and the aroma of samgyetang cycling through your dining room.

1 whole chicken (3 to 4 pounds)

1 cup cooked short-grain or glutinous rice

4 whole chestnuts, peeled

2 tablespoons ginseng powder, or 1 samgyetang broth packet

3 dried jujubes, pitted

6 garlic cloves

2 scallions, white and green parts, cut into 1-inch lengths

Kosher salt and ground black pepper

DIPPING SAUCE

¼ cup gochugaru

3 garlic cloves, minced

1 tablespoon sugar

1 teaspoon wasabi paste

½ cup chicken stock or juices from the roasted chicken

2 tablespoons soy sauce

1 tablespoon rice vinegar

1 To prepare the chicken for roasting, trim any excess fat and then remove the wing tips, as they will burn during roasting.

2 In a medium bowl, combine the rice, chestnuts, ginseng powder, jujubes, garlic, and scallions, season well with salt and pepper, and mix well. Fill the chicken cavity with the seasoned rice. Truss the chicken by tying the ends of the legs together with kitchen twine.

3 Liberally salt the whole exterior of the chicken and place it, uncovered, in the fridge for at least 4 hours or preferably overnight. This will season the bird and dry the skin, which is a critical step for achieving crisp skin.

4 When the chicken is ready to roast, preheat the oven to 350°F. Place the chicken, breast side up, on a roasting pan. Roast until an instant-read thermometer inserted into the thickest part of a thigh not touching bone registers 160°F, 1 to 1¼ hours. Remove the chicken from the oven and let rest for 10 minutes.

5 **Make the sauce:** In a small bowl, combine all the ingredients and mix well. (The sauce can be made up to a day ahead and stored in an airtight container in the fridge.)

6 Snip the twine and remove the stuffing from the chicken, then carve it! The chicken should be aromatic from the garlic and have nice golden brown skin.

KOREAN AIR BIBIMBAP WITH SAUTÉED GOCHUJANG SAUCE

대한항공 비빔밥

SERVES 4

If you've visited Korea from the United States, chances are you boarded a massive A380 belonging to Korean Air (KAL), the country's national carrier, and landed at Incheon International Airport. Now, we are hardly here to endorse KAL wholesale, and as for most airlines, we definitely have some notes. But one thing is certain: before the Ambien kicks in, we make sure to save a little consciousness for the meal service, and specifically for the Korean Air bibimbap.

Granted, the KAL BBB is not the best version of bibimbap we've ever had. It's airplane food after all. But it's a comforting spin on the stone-bowl classic that is iconic for its use of a small squeeze bottle of gochujang sauce. Deuki is adamant that the key to perfecting this deeply flavorful condiment (commonly spread over the vegetables and rice) is sautéing the gochujang with beef or pork fat, which tames the powerful jang. This recipe is a tribute to a dish that couldn't be more comforting when it's served thirty thousand feet above Alaska. The rice is the Hetbahn brand, the cooked white microwavable variety, which we recommend here for authenticity. But regular instant or steamed short-grain rice will work perfectly well too.

Note: The sauce will keep in the fridge for 3 to 4 weeks and can also be used with noodles and grilled vegetables or meat.

SAUTÉED GOCHUJANG SAUCE

1 tablespoon sesame oil

4 ounces ground beef or pork

1 small onion, diced small

6 garlic cloves, minced

1 cup gochujang

¼ cup sugar

2 tablespoons soy sauce

1 tablespoon rice vinegar

BIBIMBAP

Sesame oil, for cooking

1 bunch spinach

8 ounces mushrooms (such as shiitake, bunapi, or king oyster), trimmed

4 cups bean sprouts

1 zucchini, diced medium

Kosher salt

4 cups hot cooked rice, or 4 servings Hetbahn instant rice for a full tribute (see headnote)

4 eggs, fried (optional)

1   **Make the sauce:** In a medium saucepan, heat the oil over medium-high until it shimmers. Add the beef and cook, breaking it up and stirring often, until it is no longer pink, about 5 minutes.

2   Add the onion and garlic and sauté until light golden, 2 to 3 minutes.

3   Add the gochujang, sugar, soy sauce, and vinegar, stir well, and cook, stirring often, for 3 to 5 minutes. The sauce should be thick and a shade or two darker. Stir in 2 tablespoons or more water as needed to loosen the sauce and give it a more fluid consistency. Then remove from the heat and set aside while you make the bibimbap.

4   **Make the bibimbap:** In a large skillet, heat 1 tablespoon oil over medium-high heat until it shimmers. Add the spinach, sauté just until wilted, and transfer to a large bowl. Next sauté the mushrooms, then the bean sprouts, and finally the zucchini, sautéing each vegetable just until tender, transferring them to the bowl as they are ready, and adding oil to the pan as needed. Season the sautéed vegetables with salt.

5   Scoop the hot cooked rice into four bowls, or following the instructions on the package, cook the instant rice in a microwave. Top the rice with the sautéed vegetables and 1 tablespoon (or more) of the gochujang sauce. Finish each serving with a fried egg if desired. Serve immediately.

BUTCHER'S DOENJANG JJIGAE
BEEFY SOYBEAN PASTE STEW
된장찌개

SERVES 4

When we were working on *Koreatown*, doenjang jjigae was one of the recipes we returned to often. It was a foundational recipe, combining earthy doenjang, tofu, squash, clams, and beef. We stressed the stew's flexibility (in restaurants, it's served nearly around the clock) and double stressed that home cooks should never, *ever* substitute miso for doenjang, a staple jang (a trio of fermented soybean pastes and sauces, see page 288) widely known as "the brown tub" found at your favorite Korean market.

So why bring the recipe back for a reboot? We were wrapping up a visit and photo shoot at the Majang Meat Market in Seoul, and we found our way into the restaurant Soot Bull Tak Tak (숯불탁탁). Near the end of the meal, a bowl of a thicker, meatier doenjang jjigae than we had ever encountered arrived, and we fell hard for it. This is a recipe for a thick, meaty doenjang jjigae that we found at the restaurant, landing somewhere between a curry and a stew. It's meatier — we call for much more beef than usual — and if you can find meat scraps at your local butcher, this is a great way to use them. And as with many of our jjigae recipes, we think using the water you pour off when washing rice is better than using regular water, as it thickens the stew and adds flavor. But certainly tap water will work too.

1 tablespoon neutral cooking oil

1 pound boneless beef rib eye, short rib, or chuck, cut into 2-inch pieces

½ cup doenjang

3 tablespoons gochujang

2 tablespoons sugar

6 garlic cloves, finely minced

2 cups medium-diced Korean radish or daikon

½ cup peeled, medium-diced waxy potato (such as Yukon Gold)

½ Korean chile, thinly sliced

½ onion, thinly sliced

1 bunch scallions, white and green parts, thinly sliced

6 cups Rice Water (page 199) or water

Cooked rice, for serving

1 In a heavy medium saucepan, heat the oil over medium-high heat until it shimmers. Add the beef and sauté until fully cooked, 6 to 8 minutes.

2 Add the doenjang, gochujang, sugar, and garlic and cook in the beef fat, stirring often, for 2 to 3 minutes.

3 Add the radish, potato, chile, onion, and scallions and cook, stirring often, until thick and reduced, 3 to 5 minutes.

4 Pour in the rice water, raise the heat to high, and bring to a boil. Drop the heat to a simmer and reduce the liquid by almost half, about 15 minutes. The stew should be thick and intense, with the flavors of the beef and doenjang coming together.

5 Serve immediately, still bubbling, with a big bowl of rice.

GILGEORI TOAST
SWEET-SAVORY EGG-AND-CHEESE STREET TOAST
길거리 토스트

MAKES 1 MAJOR SANDWICH

Deuki did a VICE Munchies video for this recipe that was viewed more than 250,000 times, and the comments are wild. "This is the type of dude that I want to see on a travel show, not a random celebrity," one commenter wrote. Another noted Deuki's "battle scars," which were on full display, his forearm having had a run-in with a hot hotel pan that week. But mostly everybody was like, "This is the recipe we need," and here we are with it. In Korea, street toasts are typically sold by vendors as a quick snack for students and those on the run. It's an eggy Tilt-A-Whirl of a recipe that marries the dearly beloved sweet and savory. While variations exist (including an incredible ham and raspberry jam version at Queens in San Francisco), the constants are eggs, sugar, cabbage, and margarine. If that doesn't sound satisfying, you'll just have to trust us. And while butter works perfectly well, margarine is way more common in Korea and adds both a texture and a flavor that make this distinctly Korean.

1½ cups very thinly sliced green cabbage

4 eggs, beaten

2 tablespoons whole milk

1 tablespoon granulated sugar or light brown sugar, plus more for finishing

1 teaspoon kosher salt

2 tablespoons margarine

2 slices white sandwich bread, ¾ inch thick

2 slices American or Cheddar cheese

Ketchup, for topping

1. In a medium bowl, combine the cabbage, eggs, milk, sugar, and salt and mix well.

2. Heat a large nonstick skillet over medium heat. When the pan is hot, melt 1 tablespoon of the margarine and swirl the pan to coat the bottom. Add the egg mixture, swirl the pan to spread it evenly over the bottom, and cook until the eggs are mostly set, 5 to 6 minutes.

3. Set the bread slices side by side on top of the egg mixture and cook until the eggs are set a bit more, about 1 minute or so.

4. Using a wide spatula, flip the egg mixture and bread so the bread is now under the egg mixture. If this is too difficult, invert a large flat plate on top of the pan and flip the pan and plate together, dropping the bread and egg mixture, bread side down, onto the plate. Then slide the bread and egg mixture, bread side down, back into the pan. Place the cheese slices side by side on top of the egg mixture. Tuck in any overhanging pieces and then fold the layered egg mixture and bread in half to create a sandwich.

5. Add the remaining 1 tablespoon margarine to the pan and toast the sandwich, flipping it a couple of times, until it is light golden brown and crisp on both sides and the cheese is completely melted, about 2 minutes. Streak with ketchup and sprinkle with sugar. Serve immediately.

DEULKKAE KALGUKSU
KNIFE-CUT NOODLES IN BROTH WITH TOASTED SEAWEED AND PERILLA SEED POWDER
들깨칼국수

SERVES 4 TO 6

This simple version of kalguksu spoke to us when we were visiting Hongdukkae Handmade Noodles Soup (홍두깨 손칼국수), located in Seoul's busy Gwangmyeong Traditional Market. Kalguksu (knife-cut noodles) is sometimes called Korean fettuccine for its shape and springy quality, and at Hongdukkae Handmade, there is a real art to the process — the outcome of which draws lines of locals year-round. While the seasoning of kalguksu broth can go in many directions, we feel the addition of the uniquely nutty and herbaceous perilla seed powder brings a nice element of flavor to this beloved noodle soup. The powder, which is also used to top Matt's favorite gamjatang (pork neck stew), can be picked up in any Korean supermarket, and there's really no substitute for it. You'll sometimes find it labeled "wild sesame seed powder," which is confusing because it's not actually sesame. And even though we just said there's no good substitute for perilla seed powder, you can use ground (actual) sesame seeds for a different but still delicious result here.

NOODLES

3 cups all-purpose flour

1 cup water

1 tablespoon neutral cooking oil

1 tablespoon kosher salt

8 cups Anchovy Stock (recipe follows)

1 cup peeled, small-diced carrots

1 cup peeled, medium-diced zucchini

1 cup peeled, medium-diced russet potato

1 garlic clove, minced

2 tablespoons soy sauce, plus more to taste

½ cup perilla seed powder, for garnish

4 snack-pack-size sheets roasted and seasoned nori seaweed (kim), roughly broken up, for garnish

1 scallion, white and green parts, cut into 2-inch lengths, for garnish

1 **Make the noodles:** In a large bowl, using a fork, stir together the flour, water, oil, and salt until a workable dough begins to form. Then, using your hands, knead the dough in the bowl until it forms a smooth ball, about 5 minutes. If the dough is too sticky, add a dusting of flour. Cover the bowl with plastic wrap and refrigerate for 1 hour.

2 Remove the dough from the refrigerator, turn it out onto a floured work surface, and pat it out into a rectangle. With a rolling pin, roll out the dough into a rectangle roughly ⅛ inch thick or thinner. Dust the dough lightly with flour. Then, with a short side facing you, fold the dough into thirds, first from the bottom to the middle and then from the top to the middle. Dust lightly with flour again.

3 With a sharp knife, cut the dough lengthwise into ¼-inch-wide noodles. Divide the noodles into four to six equal portions and twirl each portion into a loose knot, adding a dusting of flour to keep the bundles from sticking together. Set aside.

4 In a large pot, bring the stock to a boil over high heat. Add the carrots, zucchini, and potato and boil until the carrots and potato are fork-tender, about 8 minutes. Halfway through the cooking, drop the noodles into the pot and boil until tender. Check for doneness to your liking.

5 When the noodles are cooked, remove the pot from the heat and stir in the garlic and soy sauce. Taste and adjust the seasoning with more soy sauce if needed.

6 Divide the noodles among four to six bowls and garnish generously with the perilla seed powder, seaweed, and scallion. Serve immediately.

MYEOLCHI YUKSU
ANCHOVY STOCK
멸치 육수

MAKES 4 CUPS

This light, quick-cooking stock can act as the base for virtually every soup and stew in the Korean kitchen. This stock will make the final product taste better, deeper, and packed with umami. Accordingly, you will find this stock used throughout the book, so if you'd like, make a large batch and freeze it in smaller portions.

Finding quality dried anchovies is as easy as finding an Asian supermarket: the skin should look healthy, more silver than gray, and the best anchovies to use for stock are at least 2 inches long. (If you're really into convenience, you can buy packages of anchovy stock base, which resemble large tea bags. Their flavor isn't quite as nuanced as our recipe, but they'll do in a pinch.) Removing the guts of the anchovy is a perfectionist step, and it's something Deuki favors because it leads to a cleaner-tasting product, but it's not strictly necessary. To do so, use your fingers to pull out the black middle section so only the head and spine of the fish remain.

Dashima is better known by its Japanese name, kombu. It's sold in dried sheets that are typically coated in a white powder. Do not wash off the powder. It aids in delivering glutamates to the stock, which adds the distinct and deep umami flavor. Finally, make sure to watch the clock, as overboiling will dampen the stock's potency.

25 dried anchovies, guts removed

¼ cup roughly chopped Korean radish or daikon

1 bunch scallions, white and green parts, cut into thirds

Two 2-inch squares kombu (dashima)

2 jalapeño or Anaheim chiles, halved lengthwise

1   In a medium saucepan, combine all the ingredients and bring to a gentle simmer over medium-high heat. Lower the heat to maintain a simmer and simmer for 15 minutes.

2   Using a fine-mesh sieve, strain the mixture into a medium-size container and discard the solids. The broth should have a cloudy, light caramel color, a deep briny taste, and a slight kick from the chiles. Use immediately, or let cool and refrigerate or freeze. The stock will keep in the refrigerator for several days or in the freezer for up to 2 months.

MEET MINGOO KANG, THE NORTH STAR OF MODERN KOREAN COOKING

Mingoo Kang is an exacting chef, first and foremost. When we entered the subterranean kitchen of Mingles, his globally celebrated Seoul restaurant in the upscale Cheongdam-dong neighborhood, a decade ago, he was quick to show us his small onggi, which was stashed in a corner of the tight space and held doenjang he was aging. We would later enjoy the first of several meals that incorporated Korean ingredients like various types of jang, seasonal produce, and local seafood and meat in the most adventurous ways, including lamb chops marinated in doenjang and tilefish pulled from the waters off Jeju Island, grilled, dressed with perilla oil, and served with bottarga.

But if you've followed his career as we have over the years, Mingoo Kang is not only the René Redzepi (the famous founder of Noma in Copenhagen) of Korea but also the Danny Meyer (daddy of the Shake Shack empire and master marketer). Seoul is seasoned with the influence of Kang. He's quickly growing a fried chicken chain, Hyodo Chicken, that transcends the sticky, sometimes one-note Korean fried "chikin" (치킨) of global beer-drinking popularity. Kang's chicken is seasoned, lightly fried, and served with fried lotus root chips and a topping of sautéed baby anchovies and shishito peppers. He's also working on a plant-based restaurant concept, and he operates the popular Hansik Goo modern Korean bistro in Hong Kong, with broad global expansion plans, including an outpost in the United States.

Americans may not know Mingoo Kang as a household name yet, but this will change with the cookbook he's writing with Nadia Cho and Joshua David Stein. *Jang* is a rigorous examination of the three foundational jangs in Korean cooking, ingredients that, of course, you see throughout this book. Doenjang, gochujang, and ganjang are a near-spiritual force that ties together many dishes in the canon of Korean cooking, and Kang and his coauthors are pushing their application to new levels.

In 2021 and 2022, we again visited Mingles, and caught up with Kang as he was overseeing the night's service. Reservations are tough to get, and Mingles is typically booked for months. And the evolution of the chef is clear from our first visit a decade earlier. One signature item on the menu is a bite of fried hagfish wrapped in a paper-thin layer of toasted kim; the dish expresses Korea's bordering ocean in a dreamy and delicious way. The closing doenjang crème brûlée with ganjang pecans and rice toasted with gochujang is called a Jang Trio and serves as a sort of mission statement for Kang's obsession with jangs. We've encountered a few jang-based desserts around the globe, and nothing comes close in terms of unusualness and pure craveability.

"Koreans didn't have a coursed-out culture," Kang says while seated in the dining room after service. A typical Korean meal may have multiple dishes on the table at once, and Kang points out how Mingles entered Seoul's fine-dining arena as a pioneer—serving menus of sequenced dishes that reflected flavors found locally. While French transplants like Pierre Gagnaire ran tasting menus in Seoul for years, serving courses heavily featuring butter and béarnaised beef, Kang went lighter and stayed true to his interests in Korean history and heritage. "The Korean table has meat, fish, and seasoned vegetables, and traditionally, Koreans didn't go for the heavy dishes," he says of his decision to buck the trend of copying the great chefs of New York and Paris with his menus. It was a tricky gambit—how to get wealthy Korean diners to spend more than $200 on courses inspired by the workaday flavors of their country. "They didn't want to spend money on Korean food, saying the fine dining was better in New York and London."

Then two things happened. First, as Korea became a wildly popular tourist destination over the past decade, American, British, and Chinese foodie tourists started to pay attention to traditional Korean cooking through a fine-dining lens. The other? "The pandemic really changed everything," Kang says. With most Koreans stuck inside the country for years, they began to look inward, acknowledging the culinary treasures locked within the peninsula's borders. At Mingles, the savory menu traditionally ends with a simple anchovy broth, in contrast to the heartier lamb or côte de boeuf typically served in a Eurocentric tasting. "This is the flavor of Korea," Kang says of the warm broth that is cold brewed and caps one of the most remarkable meals you will find anywhere in the world. "This is my home."

CHEESY CORN DOG ON A STICK
못난이 핫도그

SERVES 4

This is not a traditional American corn dog. But if you visit Korea, where foods on a stick can be seen as their own unique food group, corn dogs transcend the soggy county-fair foodstuff. These corn dogs, sometimes called Mandeugi hot dogs, are hardly traditional and don't even always include an actual hot dog, with rice cakes, fish sausages, and mozzarella cheese occasionally standing in for the "dog."

During our time in Korea, we visited various locations of the Myungrang Hotdog chain, an experience that inspired this recipe. Myungrang was founded in 2016 as a small market stall near Busan, and the business has exploded to nearly eight hundred locations in Asia and multiple shops in the United States, including Los Angeles, Atlanta, and Columbus, Ohio. At Myungrang, the crispy casing is made with rice flour, which rewards the eater with a chewy texture, and the corn dogs are streaked with the traditional mustard and ketchup, encrusted with cubes of perfectly cut potatoes, and often dusted with honey butter powder, Parmesan cheese, seaweed, and (almost universally) sugar for a sweet-savory effect. They're incredible.

In this recipe, we leave the final seasoning up to you. You'll need four skewers (or disposable wooden chopsticks) for holding the corn dogs. The simple batter can be made in minutes, and it's important to fry the corn dogs one at a time and to reserve them in a warm oven until serving.

BATTER

1 cup all-purpose flour

⅓ cup mochiko (glutinous rice flour)

3 tablespoons sugar

1 teaspoon kosher salt

1 teaspoon instant dry yeast

1 egg

½ cup warm water

2 hot dogs, halved lengthwise

4 mozzarella batons (same size as the hot dog halves), cut from a block

1 cup panko

Neutral cooking oil, for deep-frying

¼ cup sugar

FINAL SEASONINGS AND CONDIMENTS

Ramen seasoning packets, crumbled kim (seaweed), ground cinnamon, cheese powder, ketchup, mustard—be creative!

1   **Make the batter:** In a medium bowl, combine all the ingredients and mix well until smooth. Cover the bowl with plastic wrap and let sit at room temperature until the batter has almost tripled in size, 30 minutes to 1 hour.

2   Have ready four skewers. Load each skewer with a hot dog half on the bottom and a mozzarella baton on top. Be sure to leave enough of the skewer uncovered on one end to use as a "handle" for frying. Keep refrigerated until ready to batter and fry.

3   When the batter is ready, put the panko into a wide, shallow bowl. Coat the skewers with the batter until fully covered. The batter will be very thick, so you may need to use a spoon to help spread it on. One at a time, roll the batter-covered skewers in the panko and then set aside. Spread the sugar on a wide plate and set near the stove. Choose any other final dry seasonings you like and have ready on flat plates near the stove. Preheat the oven to 200°F if you want to hold the corn dogs before serving.

4   Pour the oil to a depth of 2 to 3 inches into a medium, heavy saucepan or Dutch oven and heat over medium-high heat to 350°F. When the oil is ready, holding the end of the skewer, carefully submerge the corn dog in the oil for a few seconds, then drop it into the oil and fry, turning occasionally with tongs, until golden brown, 2 to 3 minutes.

5   Using the tongs, lift the corn dog from the oil and roll it in the sugar and other dry seasonings of choice. If not serving immediately, transfer to a sheet pan or ovenproof platter and hold in the warm oven until serving. Fry the remaining corn dogs the same way. Serve hot with condiments.

KKAENNIP JEON
STUFFED AND PANFRIED PERILLA LEAVES
깻잎전

Kkaennip (known more commonly as shiso or perilla) is a prolifically grown, widely available leaf that is a cousin to mint and a staple aromatic in Korean cooking. While kkaennip can be pickled and served as a banchan, wrapped around raw fish (hwe), or served with raw fish and warm rice in a hwedupbap, it's also a supremely good choice for frying. This crispy and crunchy pancake is the sister recipe to Gochu Jeon (page 55) and can be enjoyed as a snack, set out as a hot appetizer, or served as the centerpiece dish.

On one of our visits to Seoul, we were taken to what can only be described as a bona fide temple of jeon. Kanggane Maetdol Bindaetteok (강가네맷돌빈대떡), located in Seoul's Yongsan neighborhood, consists of only a dozen or so tables and pairs the fermented rice drink makgeolli with a menu of delicately fried pancakes made of egg, potato, kimchi, scallion, squash, tofu, and whatever seasonal vegetable is available. If you make it to Seoul, do not skip it.

FILLING

8 ounces ground pork

1 small onion, diced small

2 scallions, green part only, thinly sliced

4 ounces soft tofu

1 small carrot, peeled and shredded

2 garlic cloves, minced

1 teaspoon peeled, minced fresh ginger

1½ teaspoons soy sauce

1½ teaspoons mirin

1 teaspoon kosher salt

½ teaspoon ground black pepper

24 large perilla leaves

¼ cup cornstarch

4 eggs, whisked

Neutral cooking oil

1 **Make the filling:** In a medium bowl, combine all the ingredients and mix well.

2 **Assemble the jeon:** Place 1 tablespoon of the filling in the center of each perilla leaf, fold the leaf in half, and press to seal.

3 Put the cornstarch into a small, shallow bowl. Thoroughly coat each filled leaf with cornstarch and place on a sheet pan or tray.

4 Brush each stuffed leaf with the egg, coating thoroughly.

5 Preheat the oven to 200°F. In a medium sauté pan, heat ¼ cup of oil over medium-low to medium heat until it shimmers. Working in batches to avoid crowding, panfry the stuffed leaves for about 2 minutes on each side. They should be light golden. Transfer to the sheet pan and keep warm in the oven. Repeat with the remaining stuffed leaves.

6 Serve immediately, plain or with a jeon dipping sauce.

GOCHU JEON
STUFFED AND PANFRIED CHILES
고추전

MAKES 48 SMALL STUFFED CHILES

While this rich dish slides into the jeon (pancake) family, it's closer to the American tavern snack jalapeño poppers. But regardless of what you call it, stuffing a mild pepper with pork, tofu, and classic Korean flavors before shallow frying it is a pretty great idea. This recipe is built on the technique rather than the measurements. Halve the peppers, make the filling, dust with cornstarch, brush with egg wash, fry, and repeat. It's the perfect dish to serve as an appetizer or as a main dish along with a bowl of jjigae.

FILLING

2 pounds ground pork

1 onion, diced small

1 bunch scallions, white and green parts, thinly sliced

One 14-ounce package soft tofu, drained

1 egg

½ cup peeled, shredded carrot

6 garlic cloves, minced

1-inch knob fresh ginger, peeled and minced

2 tablespoons soy sauce

2 tablespoons mirin

2 tablespoons kosher salt

2 teaspoons ground black pepper

24 Korean green chiles or Fresno or other small, mild green chiles, halved lengthwise and seeded

¼ cup cornstarch

4 eggs, whisked

Neutral cooking oil

1 **Make the filling:** In a large bowl, combine all the ingredients and mix well.

2 **Assemble the jeon:** Fill the cavity of each chile half with a spoonful of the filling.

3 Put the cornstarch into a small, shallow bowl. Thoroughly coat each filled chile with cornstarch, tapping off the excess, and place on a sheet pan.

4 Brush each stuffed chile with the egg, coating thoroughly.

5 Preheat the oven to 200°F. In a medium sauté pan, heat ¼ cup of oil over medium-low heat until it shimmers. Working in batches to avoid crowding, panfry the stuffed chiles for 2 to 3 minutes. They should be light golden brown. Transfer to a sheet pan and keep warm in the oven. Repeat with the remaining stuffed chiles.

6 Serve immediately, plain or with a jeon dipping sauce.

SPICY FRIED CHICKEN WITH BABY ANCHOVY AND CRISPY LOTUS ROOT

후라이드 치킨

On the occasions that we've made it to Seoul over the past couple of years, we've never skipped a visit to Hyodo, Mingoo Kang's fried chicken spot. Kang, who is one of the most respected fine-dining chefs in Korea (see page 48), has also made a name for himself with big ideas in fast-food fried chicken, which is known in the United States as the "other KFC," or Korean fried chicken. This is our tribute to Hyodo, which offers a slim menu of sandwiches and chicken by the piece.

Kang starts his chicken with an overnight brine in water, sugar, gochugaru, salt, onion powder, and soy sauce. The chicken is then coated in a mix of tapioca starch and flour before being deep-fried. And while the sauce is a pretty classic sticky-and-sweet Korean fried chicken sauce (yangnyeom), it's the addition of fried baby anchovies (tossed with shishito peppers and some of the yangnyeom sauce) and fried lotus root that makes this dish so incredibly delicious.

Our adaptation is made by shallow frying pounded boneless chicken thighs, similar to the method used in Japanese karaage, which is easier than frying chicken on the bone. We've included fried baby fish and lotus root. Feel free to skip either of these components – but, honestly, don't.

2 pounds boneless, skin-on chicken thighs

Neutral cooking oil

1 small lotus root, peeled and sliced into rounds

Toasted sesame seeds, for garnish

BRINE

1 cup water

1 tablespoon soy sauce

2 teaspoons sugar

2 teaspoons kosher salt

1 teaspoon gochugaru

1   **Brine the chicken:** Lightly pound the thicker end of each chicken thigh to an even thickness. Cut each thigh into two pieces if small or three pieces if large. To make the brine, in a medium bowl, whisk together the water, soy sauce, sugar, salt, and gochugaru until the sugar and salt dissolve. Submerge the chicken pieces in the brine. Cover and refrigerate overnight.

2   **Make the sauce:** The next day, in a small saucepan, combine all the ingredients and bring to a boil over medium heat, stirring frequently. Remove from the heat and reserve for coating the chicken later.

3   **Dredge the chicken:** Pour oil into a large, high-sided sauté pan to reach halfway up the sides and heat over medium-high heat to 350°F. While the oil heats, in a small bowl, whisk together the tapioca flour, salt, and pepper. In another small bowl, whisk together the eggs and water until well blended. Line a sheet pan with paper towels, then remove the chicken pieces from the brine and drain them on the towel-lined pan.

Recipe and ingredients continue

4   One at a time, dredge the chicken pieces in the flour mixture, coating well and tapping off the excess. Next, dip them in the egg mixture, letting the excess drip off. Finally, dredge them again in the flour mixture, coating completely, and then set on a large platter or sheet pan. You should be able to dredge all the chicken pieces while the oil is heating. Dredge the lotus root slices in the flour mixture only, coating them well and tapping off the excess. Set them on a separate platter.

5   **Double-fry the chicken:** Set a large wire rack on a sheet pan and set the pan near the stove. When the oil is ready, working in batches to avoid crowding, fry the chicken, turning the pieces occasionally with tongs for even cooking, until the coating is crisp but still pale, about 4 minutes. Transfer to the wire rack. Repeat with the remaining chicken, always waiting for the oil to come back up to temperature before frying the next batch. The chicken will not be fully cooked through at this stage.

6   With the oil still at 350°F and starting with the pieces that have been cooling the longest, fry the chicken in batches a second time, turning them for even cooking, until very crisp and golden brown, about 4 minutes. Transfer to the wire rack. Use a splatter screen for this second fry if you have one. The surface of the chicken will be moist after the first fry and could cause the oil to splatter.

7   Working in batches, fry the lotus root only once until crisp and golden at the edges, about 3 minutes. Transfer to the wire rack.

8   Brush the reserved sauce all over the fried chicken and lotus root. Alternatively, pile the chicken and lotus root into a large bowl, add the sauce, and toss until completely coated. You might still need a pastry brush to get into the nooks and crannies.

9   **Make the topping:** In a small bowl, stir together the soy sauce and sugar until the sugar dissolves. In a medium nonstick sauté pan, heat the oil over medium heat until it shimmers. Add the shishito peppers and cook, stirring occasionally, until they start to soften and blister, about 3 minutes. Add the anchovies and garlic and cook, stirring, until the anchovies start to crisp, about 2 minutes. Drizzle in the soy sauce mixture and stir to combine. Remove from the heat. The anchovies will crisp up as they cool.

10 Pile the sauced chicken and lotus root on a platter and top with the shishito-anchovy mixture. Sprinkle with sesame seeds and serve.

SPICY SAUCE
½ cup gochujang
½ cup rice syrup
¼ cup soy sauce
¼ cup ketchup
¼ cup water
4 garlic cloves, minced
1 tablespoon gochugaru, or more to taste

DREDGE
2 cups tapioca flour
1 teaspoon kosher salt
½ teaspoon ground black pepper
2 eggs
½ cup water

SHISHITO AND ANCHOVY TOPPING
1 tablespoon soy sauce
1 tablespoon sugar
1 tablespoon neutral cooking oil
1 cup shishito peppers
½ cup dried baby anchovies (jiri myeolchi)
2 garlic cloves, minced

Seoul's Third-Wave Coffee Scene Is Wild

It wasn't long ago that Korea was considered a backwater on the global coffee scene—laps behind Paris, Denmark, and the United States. This has changed in a big way, and for a culture that has long embraced cafés as a place not just to eat but also to socialize, Korea is now one of the fastest-growing coffee cultures in the world, with more than fifteen thousand cafés serving Seoul alone (with most having some coffee element integrated along with boba tea and baking).

"There are five really good cafés in Itaewon alone, which is a remarkable shift from even a decade ago," says Henry Park, who is seated in the Dohwa location of Fritz Coffee Company. Park is a roaster and one of the five partners of Fritz, which is one of Korea's most well-regarded brands. In the United States, you can buy bags of Fritz beans with the company's iconic fur seal imagery and bold Hangul typeface at great coffee retailers like Dayglow and Drip.

In Seoul, there's basically a third-wave shop or roaster café around every corner with—and the *Sprudge*-approved "starter kit" is being followed to a T—a Mahlkönig grinder, V60 drip station, and La Marzocco espresso machine visible in most of them. Beyond the quality of the coffee, the scene is deep into innovation of space and layout. The playful and adventurous design of these cafés left us standing and staring in doorways, drawn to buying yet another cortado or iced Einspänner, a German drink of hot espresso topped with whipped cream that has become all the rage in the city's toniest neighborhoods.

We've visited Fritz many times and sipped amazing African pour-over coffees in the walled courtyard. BK Park (no relation), Fritz's co-CEO and brand director, was a former sports journalist turned barista when he started Coffee Libre in 2009, an early pioneer in the country's nascent coffee industry, which led to the founding of Fritz in 2014. Today the Korean population is familiar with cold-brew techniques and geek-level terms like *hand brewing* and has embraced drinking good (and sometimes wildly expensive) pour-over coffee not just for connoisseurship but also as a status symbol, which factors so heavily in the culture's stratified milieu.

In and around Seoul, some house-roasted coffees are done with the greatest care (the lightest touch), and the perfectly pulled espressos are sourced from a single-origin in Guatemala or Guji. Other times, the most stunning brutalist-inspired "aesthetic" shop (as they are called) will serve something far less satisfying. But overall, and from our small sample size, the coffee scene in Seoul is one of the most swiftly advancing in the world. And when visiting Seoul, be sure to check out some of our favorite spots, including **Mesh Coffee**, **CO:LUMN**, **Lowkey**, **Matt Cafe**, **Club Espresso**, and **Tonti Coffee**.

ESPRESSO TONIC
에스프레소 토닉

SERVES 1

Matt tried to buy a coffee mug from Matt Cafe, the shop located on the ground floor of the La Marzocco Seoul headquarters and training studio in Gangnam. When he asked the barista if he could purchase it, he was asked if he was "a friend of Matt's." Deciding not to lie, he replied no — but confirmed that he, too, was a Matt. No dice. The point is, the cold espresso tonic is bonkers good. Outrageously delicious. The best cold coffee drink we've had in a long time. He had to figure out the recipe. Back in the United States, and hoping to re-create the unique blend of bright fruit, bitter tonic water, and edgy espresso, he hit up his friend Ashley Rodriguez, a writer and coffee professional running the great *Boss Barista* newsletter. Ashley helped develop this recipe, which is built around an orange simple syrup that will keep for weeks in the fridge.

2 ounces espresso (double shot)

Ice cubes

4 ounces high-quality tonic water (such as Fever-Tree)

¾ ounce Orange Simple Syrup (recipe follows)

1 rosemary sprig, for garnish

1 thin orange wheel, for garnish

1   Make the espresso however you desire. A good-quality at-home espresso machine is the best option, though this recipe will work fine with a Nespresso or other push-button machine. This step needs to be done first so the espresso can cool for at least 5 minutes. This also degases the coffee, which helps smooth out the flavor.

2   Fill a rocks glass with ice. Pour the tonic water over the ice and stir in the simple syrup.

3   Carefully pour the cooled espresso over the iced tonic water without mixing. It's helpful to have either a measuring cup or a spoon to help gently float the espresso on top. Beware: If you pour in the espresso willy-nilly, the gases in the espresso may interact with the carbonation of the tonic and cause the drink to fizz and erupt like a volcano in a science experiment.

4   Garnish with rosemary and orange wheel.

Orange Simple Syrup
오렌지 시럽

MAKES 1 CUP

In a small saucepan, combine the sugar and water over low heat and heat, stirring occasionally, until the sugar is fully dissolved. Remove from the heat and allow to cool for 10 minutes, then add the orange juice and mix well. Cover and refrigerate until cold before using. It will keep in the refrigerator for up to 1 month.

½ cup sugar (preferably Demerara)

½ cup water

½ cup fresh orange juice

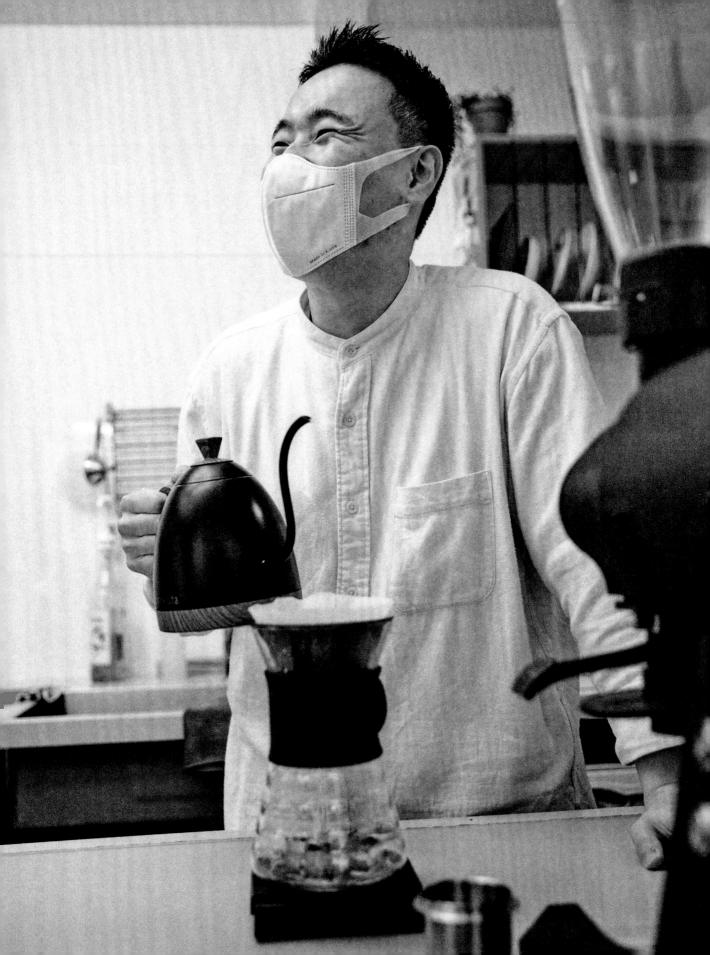

V60 POUR-OVER COFFEE
핸드드립커피

SERVES 1

Why include a pour-over coffee recipe? Coffee is one of life's great affordable luxuries, and we want to treat it with the care it deserves, not simply by winging it with a grinder and a prayer. This pour-over recipe comes from Henry Park of Fritz Coffee Company and utilizes one of our favorite hand-brewing devices, the V60, made by the Japanese company Hario. This is Park's precise recipe, and we suggest following it exactly using a gram scale, which is a worthy investment for all home cooks. Coffee culture is exploding in Korea, and precise hand brewing is the letter of the law in a growing number of the fifteen thousand cafés operating in Seoul.

18g coffee beans

Hot water, heated to 206° to 209°F, for warming and brewing

1   Grind the coffee to a medium-fine grind. (Grind it to what you think it should be, then adjust as needed according to Hario's advice: "If the brew is too weak, try a finer grind. If the water drips through the coffee too slowly, make the grind coarser.")

2   Place the V60 over a mug, insert the paper filter, and soak the filter with hot water to remove any papery taste and to warm the V60 and the mug.

3   Discard the water. Place the V60 and the mug on the scale and tare (zero out) the scale.

4   Add the ground coffee to the filter, ensuring it is evenly spread .

5   Pour enough hot water over the ground coffee to wet thoroughly, then wait for about 30 seconds. This is called the bloom.

6   Using a circular motion, slowly pour more hot water over the coffee, avoiding the edges where the ground coffee meets the paper. Stop pouring when the scale reads 290g. The whole process should take 2 minutes, 45 seconds to 3 minutes.

Exploring Seoul's Bold and Buttery Dessert Scene with Nünchi's Lexie Park

On a gray November morning, Lexie Park meets us at Cafe Onion Anguk, a branch of the popular Seoul-based bakery chain tucked just off the touristy Changgyeonggung Palace. Park, who is best known as the Los Angeles–based jelly cake innovator and social media star Nünchi, doesn't often give interviews, and our meeting was set up only after an introduction from a mutual friend and a series of spirited Kakao exchanges discussing eating horse on Jeju Island, bad pizza in Korea, and thirst-trap LA chefs. We knew Park was our kind of person and had soon arranged to jump around Seoul for the day to answer a single question: What is up with these sometimes confusing, oftentimes remarkable, rapidly expanding Korean bakeries that have taken over the urban landscape? Ever since the boom of mega café chains like Tous Les Jours and Paris Baguette first in Korea, and later in the United States, we've been fascinated. We've been intrigued by the evolution away from Frankenpastries (hot dogs tucked into sweet and yeasty breads) toward world-class viennoiserie and a style of dessert that is completely new. But first, while sharing a powdered sugar–crowned pandoro and other modern Korean pastries, we wanted to take down Park's story.

She grew up working in her family's business in downtown Los Angeles's garment district. Days were long, and Park recounts hawking clothing on the street as a kid. While her dreams of attending arts school eluded her, she stuck with fashion and eventually worked for Opening Ceremony, a brand founded by Asian Americans, before launching her own brand, Phlemuns Nonbasics, in 2018.

It was through these fashion jobs that Park was introduced to many people in the chef world, including acclaimed *Top Chef* winner Mei Lin, then of the restaurant Nightshade. Park would ask the chef to help her practice her knife skills, and Lin would gladly set her up with a box of onions to peel. Trips to the farmers' market certified her interest in working with the stellar California produce, and before long, Park's mind had flipped into food entrepreneur-artist mode. "I was really into fermentation and preservation, and Jell-O was used as a preservative back in the day," she says. "It got me thinking, 'How is this brand on every grocery-store shelf in America taking up so much space?'"

After spending time with Nightshade pastry chef Max Boonthanakit and scouring YouTube tutorials, Park landed on a form and aesthetic that was originally intended as a long-term art project. Nünchi was born with a jelly cheesecake on July 4, 2019, exploding online (her social media following has ballooned to the hundreds of thousands) and offline (The Weeknd was photographed with a Nünchi cake at the Super Bowl). The Korean word nunchi doesn't have a direct translation in English, but it means something along the lines of being aware of your surroundings and picking up on things that aren't said, which plays a big role in Korean culture.

Per our request, and saving room for a barbecue feast at Mongtan later in the evening, we hopped into a cab and were off. Along with her partner, Willy, we hoped to try some of Seoul's more interesting desserts. Our first stop was Passion 5, a concept café run by the SPC Group (the conglomerate behind Paris Baguette). What are the five passions, you may wonder? Café, bakery, patisserie, chocolate, and, well, the passion from the company's pâtissiers. But the baking was no joke, and the Baumkuchen display was a thing of beauty: on view behind glass, a giant rotating spit of cake (not unlike a rotating al pastor at an East LA taco truck) made of more than twenty layers of cake batter, each painstakingly baked to create a gorgeous, multilayered dessert.

Park and Willy went with a lemon cake (posing as a lemon), a chocolate tart, and a Swiss roll. The lemon cake and Swiss roll were the big hits, while the tart was underwhelming. The vibe was polished, though corporate. It is profound how much butter is now used in modern Korean baking. When we first started writing about Korea just over a decade ago, it was only a tiny part of the food culture. Today, the streets around Seongsu and Apgujeong are perfumed with the smells of toasted pastry butter, and you are as likely to stumble upon a decent kouign-amann as you are a tray of kimbap.

While living in Seoul for a couple of months, Park started doing her own jelly cake pop-ups and found sourcing difficult. "Philadelphia cream cheese is so different," she says. "The cheese found in Seoul is way sweeter, more brittle, chalkier, and smooth, and we were having a hard time working with it." Back on the crawl, we wanted to know how the pastries stack up to those of Japan, which has long been heralded as home to pastry on par with France and the United States. "I have a lot of Korean pride, and I hate the battle between Korea and Japan when it comes to these kinds of things. But Japan just has so much history, and [Japanese bakers] have been able to craft and perfect all of these things, evolving slowly, [while] Korea is fast-paced and always looking for the cool thing, which is also really cool to see."

We move on to our last dessert stop before heading to barbecue (food writing, gotta love it) and are introduced to what many have said is the best ice cream in Korea. Zenzero is known for adventurous flavors folded into a perfect eggless gelato form. The salted caramel is flavored with a type of seaweed called gamtae, and the shop has been known to offer a rotation of vegetable scoops like sweet pea and cabbage. On our visit, we scooped up a classic rice flavor, fig mascarpone, and the gamtae caramel. The mascarpone would fit in perfectly in a piazza in Milan. The caramel was on the level of ice cream master Van Leeuwen in New York.

The point is, Korea's dessert scene has exploded, and the future is bright and buttery. And while Japan grabs headlines with a well-seasoned culture of mastering lamination and even Western fruit pies, Korea's very young bakers are showing up each and every morning.

"There is no place I'd rather be working than in Seoul," Park confides about her possible full-time future in Korea. And if we were to apply nunchi to the situation, we'd intuit that this move may happen sooner rather than later.

TTEOKGALBI
SEASONED BEEF PATTIES (THE KOREAN HAMBURGER)
떡갈비

SERVES 4 TO 6

Matt has been thinking about tteokgalbi (rough translation: "rice cake of beef") since his first interaction with the tender and sweet meat patty that is widely beloved in Korea (and given much less attention in the United States). It was his first trip to Seoul in 2013, and his kind host had taken him to lunch at one of the city's most posh and modern tasting-menu restaurants. With the modernist early courses behind them, a lightly grilled patty of ground short rib seasoned with orchard fruits and soy sauce arrived with great ceremony. It was tteokgalbi, and all Matt could think was, "Wait, a Korean hamburger is stealing the show?" It was delicious, no doubt, but not earth-shattering as a dish reflecting the Korean food canon.

Since then, in Korea, tteokgalbi has grown wildly popular, and it can be found in fast-casual restaurants and in multipacks in markets. The dish was originally presented to the royal court during the Joseon period (1392–1897) – a time during which meat was extremely rare and needed to stretch. Tteokgalbi first popped up on modern menus in the Songjeong neighborhood in Gwangju in the 1970s, and today there's a street of tteokgalbi sellers offering versions made with pork and duck meat. We tried a really good, oversize one at Mangwon Market in Seoul.

Here's our interpretation, and it's honestly become a big hit with our friends – and a great dish to make when kids are at the dinner table: mild, sweet, and easy to prepare with ground meat and basic pantry ingredients. We call for chuck, but in Korea, this is often made using ground short rib, so ask your butcher to grind you some.

2 pounds ground chuck or short rib (80/20)

1 small white onion, grated

6 garlic cloves, minced

4 scallions, white and green parts, chopped

1-inch knob fresh ginger, peeled and minced

5 tablespoons soy sauce

2 tablespoons sugar

2 tablespoons mirin

2 tablespoons sesame oil

1 teaspoon kosher salt

1 teaspoon ground black pepper

1 tablespoon neutral oil, for cooking

1   In a large bowl, combine the ground chuck, onion, garlic, scallions, ginger, soy sauce, sugar, mirin, sesame oil, salt, and pepper and mix together gently. Divide the meat mixture into eight equal portions and roll each portion into a round meatball. Place the meatballs on a plate, cover, and refrigerate for 30 minutes.

2   In a large skillet, heat the oil over medium heat until it shimmers. Working in batches if needed to avoid crowding, add the meatballs, spacing them well apart, and flatten slightly to about 1½-inch thickness. Cook until a brown crust forms on the bottom, 3 to 4 minutes. Flip the meatballs and brown on the second side, 3 to 4 minutes.

3   Flip the meatballs again, then turn down the heat to medium-low and cover the pan. Cook, flipping them halfway through cooking, for 8 minutes. The beef should now be cooked to medium.

4   Finally, uncover the skillet and raise the heat to medium. The juices in the pan that will thicken and lightly glaze the meatballs. Continue cooking, flipping periodically, until the meatballs are cooked through, juicy, and nicely browned, 2 to 3 minutes longer. Serve immediately.

MAYAK GYERANBAP

EXTREMELY ADDICTING SOY SAUCE–MARINATED EGGS WITH RICE

마약 계란밥

SERVES 4

These sweet, garlicky, soy-infused eggs can be loosely translated as "drug eggs," so named because of their magnetic craveability, a quality they share with their spiritual brethren, Taiwanese tea eggs. The eggs are cooked to a soft and yolky consistency and served over rice as a full meal (as suggested here) or by themselves for a robust snack.

Note: To make the eggs easier to peel, add a couple of spoonfuls of vinegar (any kind) and pinches of kosher salt to the boiling water before adding the eggs.

8 eggs

MARINADE

1 cup soy sauce

¼ cup water

⅓ cup loosely packed brown sugar

2 tablespoons granulated sugar

6 garlic cloves, minced

1-inch knob fresh ginger, peeled and minced

4 scallions, green part only, thinly sliced

2 tablespoons sesame seeds

1 red or green Korean chile, thinly sliced, with seeds

1 tablespoon sesame oil

½ cup crushed roasted nori seaweed (kim)

4 cups cooked rice

Sesame oil, for drizzling

4 snack-pack-size sheets roasted nori seaweed (kim), crumbled

1   Have ready a large bowl of ice water. Fill a medium saucepan with water and bring to a boil over medium heat. Add the eggs and cook for exactly 6 minutes. Scoop the eggs out of the pan and shock them in the ice water. When the eggs are cool, remove them from the bowl, discard the water, and dry the bowl. Peel the eggs and return them to the bowl.

2   **Make the marinade:** In a medium bowl, whisk together the soy sauce, water, both sugars, garlic, ginger, scallions, sesame seeds, chile, oil, and seaweed until the sugars dissolve and all the ingredients are well mixed. Pour the marinade over the eggs, cover the bowl, and refrigerate for 24 to 48 hours.

3   Divide the rice among four bowls. Cut the marinated eggs in half and add two halves to each bowl of rice. Spoon one-fourth of the marinade over the eggs and rice, then drizzle with the oil and sprinkle with the seaweed.

The Euljiro Eulogies

Jason Kim, who runs the thorough and iconoclastic website and Instagram account My Korean Eats, has taken us for a plate of steamed whole sea bream rimmed with half shells of fresh abalone at one of Seoul's quietly dying restaurants. The owner, a woman well into her sixties, was the only employee in the single-room space that was fashioned more like a street-level apartment. Kim tells us she even sleeps there on an air mattress some nights after service. The restaurant, which has been operating since the 1980s, is dwarfed by modern skyscrapers crowded with neon lettering announcing a telecom or entertainment conglomerate within. For years, Kim has been covering the aging population running many of Korea's restaurants and the rapid gentrification closing in on these legacy institutions, and there's no clearer example of the fading out of old-school pojangmachas (tented restaurants) and jjigae sellers than the Euljiro neighborhood. He's chronicled their demise with passion and palpable anger.

"One of the most egregious things I've ever witnessed in my life [is] happening right now to my beloved Eulji OB Bear, Korea's first and foremost draft beer and nogari pub that's been [around] for over 40 years," Kim writes in an impassioned website post about a now-closed establishment. In it, Kim, a former line cook and radio show host, flips the bird at construction workers gutting an evicted space. Eulji OB Bear operated for more than four decades near the Euljiro 3-ga Station on the busy Seoul metro lines 2 and 3. It was a place for the neighborhood electronics and iron workers to congregate after long shifts, sipping cheap, ice-cold domestic beer and snacking on nogari (dried pollack) dipped in a type of crimson chojang (gochujang plus vinegar) or mayonnaise.

But on April 21, 2022, an eviction notice initiated by the building's landlord was upheld, and the pub was forced to close forever. Kim points out that the neighborhood's winding alleyways lined with shuttered electronics shops, reminders of Korea's tech boom in the 1980s, were taken over in the late 2010s by a younger generation opening bars and restaurants in the style of downtown Los Angeles and Brooklyn's now fully gentrified Williamsburg neighborhood. With this influx came changing landlord demands and new condo construction, marketing a creative and cool life in Hip-jiro, a portmanteau of "hip" and "Euljiro."

The legacy restaurants haven't gone quietly. Protests are a near-monthly occurrence, and on a weekend night in 2022, we came across Eulji OB Bear's former owner, Soo-young Choi, participating in a demonstration—giving speeches and drinking a little, too, in a show of solidarity for the neighborhood's evicted taverns and restaurants. While Kim has moved back to the United States for now, he's still keeping tabs on Seoul's rapid transformation. Follow him at @MyKoreanEats for the continued eulogies for Seoul's dying neighborhoods.

을지OB베어와 함께하는 음악회
조물주 위에 건물주? 만선호프! 노가리골목 독점을 중단하라!
폭력적인 강제집행 자행한 건물주 만선호프 규탄한다!
서울시와 중구청은 서울미래유산 보존을 위해 을지OB베어 사태 해결하라!
만선호프! 가리골목 독점을 중단하라!
을지OB베어는 빼앗길 수 없는 들의 가게입니다.
을지로13길 12
김길성 구청장님! 을지OB베어 사태는 중구의 1호 민원입니다

The 17 Best Things We Ate in Seoul and around Korea

While reporting for this book, we traveled all over Korea, from Jeju, Gwangju, Gangwon, and Jeolla to walking around the neighborhoods of Seoul. We drank incredible hand-brewed coffee and had new adventures with persimmon, doenjang, hotteok, dubu, hay-smoked kalbi, and more. Here are some of our favorites.

Seoul Seolleongtang
Yeongdong Seolleongtang
24 Gangnam-daero 101an-gil,
Seocho-gu, Seoul

Espresso Tonic
Matt Cafe
42 Hakdong-ro 50-gil,
Gangnam-gu, Seoul

Peanut Butter Sandwich
on Milk Bread
Meal° (Meal-do)
96, Seongdong-gu,
Wangsimni-ro, Seoul

Mountain Chicken Soup in
Gangwon-do
Gakdugol
Seoraksan National Park

Kimbap with Truffled
Tuna Mayo
Hojokban
39 Eonju-ro 164-gil, Sinsa-dong,
Gangnam-gu, Seoul

Big Boy Kalbi Rib and All the
Sauces
Mongtan
50 Baekbeom-ro 99-gil,
Yongsan-gu, Seoul

Grilled Persimmon
with Dubu Sauce
Buto
32 Hannam-daero 27ga-gil,
Hannam-dong, Seoul

Hotteok Stuffed with Japchae
Namdaemun Market
21 Namdaemunsijang 4-gil,
Jung-gu, Seoul

Jangs Trio Dessert
Mingles
19 Dosan-daero 67-gil, 2F,
Gangnam-gu, Seoul

Pepperoni Pizza
Bums Pizza
62-2 Hangangno-dong,
Yongsan-gu, Seoul

Ice Cream
Zenzero
Seolleung-ro 126-gil,
Gangnam-gu, Seoul

Basket of Jeon
Kanggane Maetdol Bindaetteok
27 Daesagwan-ro 24-gil,
Yongsan-gu, Seoul

Fried Chicken Basket with
Fried Baby Anchovies and
Lotus Root
Hyodo Chicken
20 Daesagwan-ro, Hannam-dong,
Yongsan-gu, Seoul

Temple Dubu
Hwaeomsa Buddhist Monastery
Yeongiam-gil, Masan-myeon,
Gurye-gun, Jeollanam-do

Pour-Over Coffee
Mesh
43 Seoulsup-gil, Seongsu-dong,
Seongdong-gu, Seoul

Ssam Bap
Nanpo Hannam
18 Itaewon-ro 49-gil,
Hannam-dong, Seoul

Budae Jjigae
Bada Sikdang
18, Itaewon-ro, 49-gil,
Yongsan-gu, Seoul

Hotteok

Pepperoni Pizza

Seoul Seolleongtang

Big Boy Kalbi Rib

SPAGHETTI ALLE VONGOLE
봉골레 스파게티

SERVES 3 OR 4

This? Here? Okay, hear us out. During our travels in and around Korea, it became clear that Italian food — mostly notably pasta — has exploded in popularity for both restaurant diners and home cooks across the country. Restaurants in Busan, Gwangju, and Seoul sell a pure escape to the Italian Riviera through a bowl of linguine with pesto. But for home cooks, it can be challenging. Quality canned tomatoes can be hard to find in Korea, and when you do spot them in a luxury food hall like Gourmet 494, they can be expensive. Pine nuts? Forget about it. The work-around is spaghetti alle vongole, a dish cemented in the Italian canon that, when prepared in Korea, utilizes many ingredients that are commonly found local items: clams, garlic, parsley, gochugaru for a warming spiciness, and soju in place of white wine, which adds an element of depth. You can, of course, sub in white wine for the soju and chile flakes for the gochugaru. But this Korean-style version is really great as written.

Kosher salt

8 ounces dried spaghetti

¼ cup extra-virgin olive oil

4 to 6 garlic cloves, minced

½ teaspoon gochugaru

2 pounds littleneck or Manila clams, scrubbed thoroughly

½ cup soju

2 tablespoons finely chopped fresh flat-leaf parsley, or a handful of arugula

1 Bring a large pot of water to a boil over high heat. Season it well with salt, add the pasta, and cook, stirring occasionally, until 1 to 2 minutes shy of al dente, according to the package instructions. Drain the pasta, reserving ½ cup of the cooking water, and set the pasta and water aside separately.

2 While the pasta is cooking, begin making the sauce. In a Dutch oven or other large, heavy pot, heat the oil over medium heat until it shimmers. Add the garlic and gochugaru, turn down the heat to medium-low, and cook, stirring often, until fragrant, 2 to 3 minutes.

3 Add the clams and soju, stir well, and raise the heat to medium. Cover and steam until all the clams have fully opened, about 5 minutes. Using tongs, transfer the clams to a plate, discarding any that failed to open.

4 Add the cooked pasta to the sauce and toss and stir until evenly coated and al dente, using the reserved cooking water to loosen the sauce as needed. Return the clams to the pot, add the parsley, and toss and stir until well mixed. Serve immediately.

DOOBYDOBAP IS TEACHING THE INTERNET TO COOK MORE KOREAN

Tina Choi is the Seoul-based genius behind one of our favorite YouTube food accounts, Doobydobap, and her work represents the area of greatest momentum for Korean food right now: social media video like TikTok, Instagram Reels, and YouTube. While we were writing *Koreatown* back in 2013, there were only a handful of online resources available in English to learn about Korean cooking. New York–based author and creator Maangchi was and is the grande dame of Korean food content, but she was really it at the time.

But today, Choi streams weekly to a *massive* audience she's built in just a few years (nearly four million subscribers on YouTube alone). She was born in Korea, grew up in Canada, attended boarding school in Connecticut, and later studied food science at Cornell. She currently lives in Korea and the United States, and she uses both countries (and varying kinetic cultures) as the backdrop for her personal and effortlessly cool dispatches about her life in and out of the kitchen. Among her hits are "stand-and-stir" kitchen tutorials for garlic fried chicken, pig's trotter ragù, rabokki (spicy rice cakes and ramen), and cheesy kimchi rice balls, along with personal stories, thoughtful meditations, and even comedy. The dishes, like many recipes in this book, are more modern than traditional, though they are rooted in the classic Korean kitchen moves of grandmas and aunts.

"I try to keep it very raw and very real," says Choi of her style over lunch at Momofuku Noodle Bar. Choi was inspired by Ina Garten, Alton Brown, and Bill Nye the Science Guy, and her ease and brilliantly comedic timing make her videos addictive and incredibly popular with a young and inquisitive millennial and Gen Z following (and sure enough, two different fans stopped her for selfies during our short visit).

But Choi remains clear that she has a lot of growing to do in the kitchen and hesitates at the mention of her cooking skills. Though she's more than proficient when cooking a robust winter jjigae, giving a tip for searing dubu (tofu), or making up a prawn toast snack, she's adamant that's she not a cooking authority. "I can write, I can cook, I can talk a little bit," she says modestly. "I'm really still trying to find my way as a cook and find my style of cooking." Her cooking style sometimes leans light and flavorful—shying away from heavy barbecues—and sometimes is a true marriage of the United States and Korea. Pizza and furikake-dusted bagels get as much play as soondubu jjigae (tofu stew).

"I used to hide from who I was, but now I am loud and proud," Choi says when asked about her journey to one of Korean food's most prominent global ambassadors. She's learning to live as a clear public figure. Choi's rise is nearly parallel, in timing, with the rise of Korean food globally.

She credits K-pop group Blackpink and the popularity of Korean dramas like *Squid Game*. But if you've been paying attention, broadcast television is dead—long live TikTok, a platform Choi has employed with extreme success, and one she has been using shrewdly while launching her first restaurant in Seoul, a casual, tasting menu spot called Mija. "I get recognized more in Italy than in Korea or the United States." Choi laughs. When lunch ends and we're leaving the restaurant, she doesn't seem to notice the delighted fan snapping her photo as she walks by.

SOONDUBU SHAKSHUKA
SPICY SOFT TOFU AND EGGS
순두부 샥슈카

SERVES 2

This recipe, a combination of spicy tofu stew (soondubu jjigae) and Northern African–Mediterranean simmered eggs that becomes its own unique thing, comes from Tina Choi, one of our favorite recipe developers on the internet and a rising star in Food Media™. When we asked her about collaborating on a recipe, she was in the midst of opening her first restaurant, called Mija, in Seoul – a process that she documented with wild candor on her very popular YouTube page.

Note: You must prepare the aioli at least 30 minutes before serving to allow time for it to set, so make it first.

⅓ cup neutral cooking oil

¼ cup finely diced onion

2 scallions, green and white parts, thinly sliced, plus more for garnish

2 garlic cloves, thinly sliced

½ cup diced oyster mushrooms

2 tablespoons gochugaru

1 tablespoon soy sauce

¼ cup water

1 to 2 tablespoons fish sauce

4 eggs

Tofu Aioli (recipe follows; see Note)

1 In a medium skillet, heat the oil over medium-high heat until it shimmers. Add the onion, scallions, garlic, and mushrooms and sauté until the onion is translucent and the mushrooms are golden brown, 3 to 4 minutes.

2 Drop the heat to low, add the gochugaru, and stir the ingredients together quickly so the gochugaru does not burn. The oil should turn a scarlet hue at this point.

3 While the oil is still hot, drizzle in the soy sauce and let it burn slightly. This step imparts more depth and smokiness to the chile oil.

4 Add the water and deglaze the pan, stirring to dislodge all the browned bits (the fond) from the pan's bottom. Season the mixture with the fish sauce, using as much as needed to make it slightly saltier than to your liking, as the eggs will temper the saltiness.

5 Once the mixture comes to a simmer, use the back of a spoon to create four evenly spaced hollows in the mushroom mixture. Carefully crack an egg into each hollow. Cover the pan and cook over low heat until the whites of the eggs have set and the yolks are still runny, about 7 minutes.

6 Dollop a generous amount of the aioli next to the eggs, garnish with scallions, and serve straight from the skillet.

Tofu Aioli
두부 아이올리 소스

MAKES ABOUT 1 CUP

1 In a blender, combine the tofu, oil, vinegar, garlic, salt, and a drizzle of honey (if using) and blend until smooth.

2 Transfer to a bowl, cover, and place in the fridge for at least 30 minutes to firm up before serving. Leftover aioli will keep refrigerated for up to a week.

12 ounces firm tofu

½ cup neutral cooking oil

2 tablespoons rice vinegar

1 garlic clove

1 tablespoon kosher salt

Honey, for seasoning (optional)

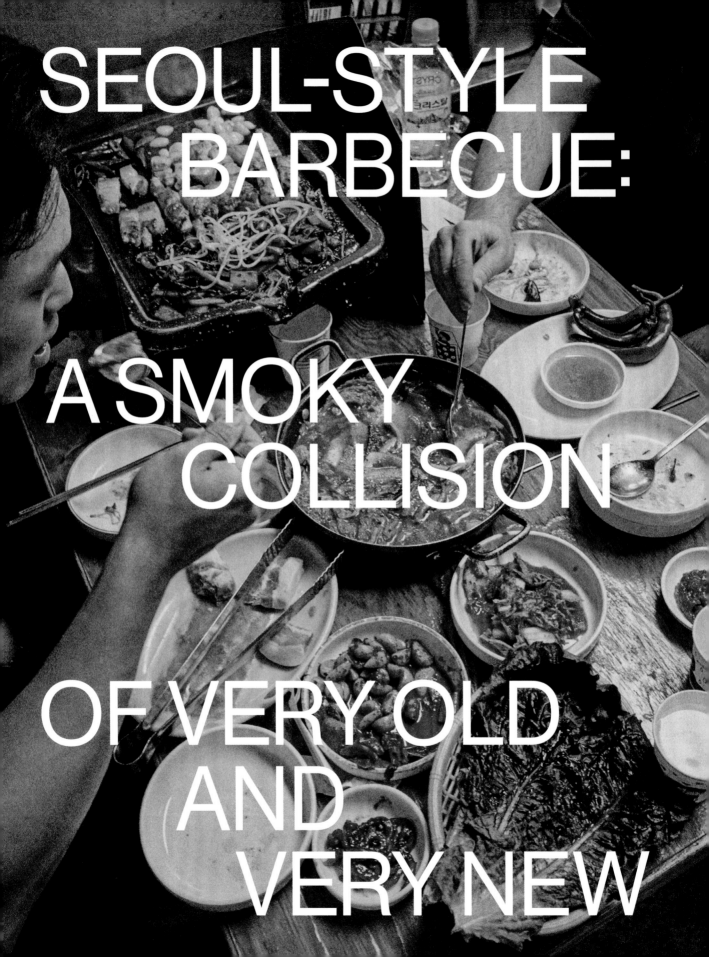

SEOUL-STYLE BARBECUE:

A SMOKY COLLISION

OF VERY OLD AND VERY NEW

In the United States, Korean-style barbecue restaurants are still the most frequent doorways diners walk through when being introduced to Korean food. We love many aspects of the searing of marinated beef and pork on hot grills, and Deuki ran a Korean barbecue restaurant in New York City for several years where he took particular joy in serving K-food newbies each and every night—and there were some late ones for our hero the chef.

While recipes for the greatest hits of kalbi, bulgogi, and the like fill a number of books, we wanted instead to show a snapshot of our recent barbecue experiences in Seoul, one that acknowledges the past and tips to the future of Korean barbecue. In Seoul, thousands of restaurants devoted to specific cuts of meat, such as samgyeopsal (pork belly) and chadol (beef brisket), operate nearly around the clock. Although the fundamental principles are the same—have meat, have fire, have side dishes, commence feast—we've seen things to make us rethink nearly every aspect of the barbecue setup. As you walk around the busy streets of Seongsu and Apgujeong, amazing innovation—for example, taking kimchi and making it into a frozen side dish—is clear. Yet the decades-long perfection of the craft is also apparent when visiting decades-old kalbi restaurants.

Think of this chapter as a guide to cooking a modern Korean barbecue feast, which naturally also looks back to the past for inspiration. We've featured only two meat recipes, a hay-smoked beef short rib and a backyard gochujang BBQ pork rib, along with a number of unique banchan recipes that we think deserve a place in your next Korean barbecue spread. We've offered three ways to make ssamjang, the long-loved classic Korean barbecue sauce, presented here with a modern twist. There's also an icy radish kimchi granita, and we've landed on a method for taking your used barbecue grill pan or grate (with all those amazing, scorched meat bits) and utilizing it to make the best post-barbecue bokkeumbap (fried rice).

HUNJE UDAE KALBI
SMOKED GIANT SHORT RIBS
훈제 갈비

SERVES 4

At Mongtan, the multi-hour-long waits are famous – almost as famous as the fire-and-smoke show that greets diners as they enter one of Seoul's most popular modern barbecue restaurants, located near Samgakji Station in Itaewon. Of all the incredible dishes we tasted in Korea, none showed us a new wave of Korean barbecue as much as this "dinosaur" short rib that was skillfully marinated (and then smoked over hay). We knew we had to develop a recipe.

The key here is to let the marinade hit the meat for only a short period – up to eight hours, tops. This flavor is not the overpowering orchard fruits of a traditional American-style kalbi. It's also very lightly smoked, only kissed with the woody vapor for ten minutes at the end of the grilling process. The result is amazing – not quite Korean kalbi, not quite Hill Country brisket, but a marriage of the two.

MARINADE

½ small onion

½ Asian pear

½ apple

6 garlic cloves

½ cup diced canned pineapple, drained

½ cup soy sauce

⅔ cup firmly packed brown sugar

¼ cup Korean corn syrup (mulyeot)

2 tablespoons honey

1 tablespoon sesame oil

1 teaspoon toasted sesame seeds

1½ cups water

One 3- to 4-pound bone-in rack of beef short ribs

Kosher salt

8 ounces rice straw or hay, for smoking

1   **Make the marinade:** In a blender or food processor, combine all the ingredients and blend until smooth. Transfer to a bowl, cover, and refrigerate for 2 to 4 hours.

2   Cut the short rib rack into individual ribs by slicing between the bones, then trim off any excess fat. Transfer the ribs to a large bowl or ziplock bag, pour the marinade over the ribs, and mix to coat evenly. Cover the bowl or seal the bag and marinate overnight in the refrigerator. (Do not marinate longer than overnight. You do not want the ribs to be heavily marinated, which creates kalbi. The seasoning must be present, but you want the flavor of beef and smoke to be the star.)

3   Prepare a charcoal or gas grill for direct cooking over medium heat. To check if it's ready, place your hand 6 inches above the grate; you should be able to withstand the heat for only about 5 seconds before pulling away.

4   Remove the ribs from the marinade and pat them dry. Season lightly with salt. Place the ribs on the grate over low to medium heat and cook until a meat thermometer inserted into thickest part of a rib not touching bone registers 120°F, 20 to 25 minutes. Transfer the ribs to a sheet pan or platter and set aside.

5   Lift the grill grate and add the straw in clumps directly to the charcoal. It will catch fire quickly. When the flames die down and the straw starts to smoke, replace the grate, top with the ribs, and close the grill lid. Let the ribs smoke and cook until when you test again with the thermometer, it registers 140°F for medium, 10 to 15 minutes longer.

6   Transfer the ribs to a carving board and let rest for 20 to 30 minutes.

7   Remove the bone from each rib, slice the meat into thin steak cuts, and serve.

3 SSAMJANGS: A SPREAD FOR EVERY MOOD
DIPPING SAUCE, SPREAD, AND UTILITY PLAYER
쌈장

Ssamjang is a hearty spread that you will find on the table at any Korean barbecue restaurant. The word *ssam* means "wrapped," and *jang* means "thick sauce," so by definition, this is a spread to be slathered on lettuce or perilla leaves that are then wrapped around hunks of grilled meat, kimchi, and any of the banchan you want to include. It's a warhorse of a condiment. In *Koreatown*, we published a single ssamjang recipe, and it was honestly really bomb. The flavor was complex and layered, something we had trouble describing. In fact, we sat around the test kitchen for a good fifteen minutes throwing out words like *umami*, *sweet*, and *nutty* before settling on *essential*. That is to say, all Korean barbecue tables need a homemade version.

Commercial ssamjang is widely available at Korean markets (it's the green plastic tub in the jang aisle). It's not bad, and it's what you will find at the larger Korean barbecue restaurants. But like many condiments in the Korean kitchen, a homemade version is fuller in flavor. Here we have developed three versions of ssamjang, each with a unique approach, but all are flavor-packed condiments that can live on your table and in your fridge for weeks. One version leans into nuts and seeds (we call for walnuts, but shelled pistachios work really well, too), while another is more fruit-forward. Finally, there's a beefy version that we even shocked ourselves with. It's so good, we couldn't stop spooning it into our mouths. Enjoy your ssamjang making.

Nuts and Seeds
In a small bowl, combine all the ingredients and mix well.

Apple and Onion
In a small bowl, combine all the ingredients and mix well.

The Plot Twist: Meat!
1   In a medium skillet, heat the oil over medium heat until it shimmers. Add the onion, scallion, and garlic and cook, stirring often, until translucent, 2 to 3 minutes. Add the pork and cook, breaking it up and stirring often, until fully cooked, 5 to 7 minutes.

2   Add the gochujang, doenjang, soy sauce, rice syrup, and sugar, stir well, and simmer, stirring occasionally, for 1 to 2 minutes to blend the flavors. Remove from the heat, allow to cool for a couple of minutes, and fold in the mayonnaise. Serve at room temperature.

Nuts and Seeds
1 cup soy sauce
¼ cup water
⅓ cup loosely packed brown sugar
6 garlic cloves, minced
1-inch knob fresh ginger, minced
2 tablespoons sugar
4 scallions, thinly sliced
2 tablespoons chopped walnuts
2 tablespoons sesame seeds
1 red or green Korean chile, thinly sliced, with seeds
1 tablespoon sesame oil
½ cup crushed roasted seaweed (kim)

Apple and Onion
½ onion, grated and strained
½ tart apple, peeled and grated
½ green Korean chile, thinly sliced, with seeds
3 tablespoons doenjang
1 tablespoon gochujang
2 tablespoons sugar
2 tablespoons roasted soybean powder
1 tablespoon minced garlic
2 tablespoons sesame oil

The Plot Twist: Meat!
2 tablespoons neutral cooking oil
½ onion, diced small
3 tablespoons thinly sliced scallion, white and green parts
1 tablespoon minced garlic
4 ounces ground pork or beef
1 tablespoon gochujang
3 tablespoons doenjang
1 tablespoon soy sauce
1 tablespoon rice syrup
2 tablespoons sugar
1 tablespoon mayonnaise

YANGNYEOM GANJANG
BEEF BARBECUE DIPPING SAUCE
양념간장

MAKES 2 CUPS

This sweet and spicy sauce derives from a question we pondered a bit: ssamjang, the traditional Korean barbecue condiment, is great, but is there more? The answer is yes, in the form of this dip that evolved from Deuki's work running the New York City barbecue restaurant Kang Ho Dong Baekjeong. The sauce can be served in individual bowls for guests to use for dunking their meat. This is a great utility sauce, and it's incredible with any unmarinated grilled meat, but particularly chadol (thinly sliced beef brisket). It is ideally assembled the day before serving, minus the wasabi, which is added just before eating. The wasabi is critical in unlocking the sauce's push and pull between sweetness and refreshing spice, so do not skip it.

½ cup light soy sauce

¼ cup Korean honey powder or sugar

¼ cup cider vinegar

¼ cup rice syrup

¼ cup water

½ small onion, diced

1 serrano or jalapeño chile, seeded and thinly sliced

1 teaspoon wasabi paste

1 In a small bowl, combine the soy sauce, honey powder, vinegar, rice syrup, water, onion, and chile and mix well. Cover and refrigerate for at least 1 hour and preferably for 24 hours before serving. This step is important, as it allows the flavors to meld.

2 When ready to serve, stir the wasabi into the sauce. The sauce will keep in an airtight container in the refrigerator for up to several weeks.

YANGPA KIMCHI
WHOLE ONION KIMCHI
양파김치

SERVES 4

We encountered this kimchi banchan at Seoul's amazing Mongtan in Samgakji. Doing the whole onion, kimchi-style, was new to us and the Korean restaurant scene, and the result fits perfectly into any barbecue plans: easy to make ahead and perfectly paired with smoky and fatty meats. More of a hybrid kosher pickle than traditional cabbage kimchi, it is slightly sour and without any overpowering allium flavor. It's one of our favorite discoveries. Enjoy with any grilled meats or Korean barbecue feast.

4 medium white or
   Spanish onions

MARINADE

1 apple, peeled, cored, and
   coarsely chopped

1-inch knob fresh ginger, peeled
   and coarsely chopped

¼ cup gochugaru

½ cup fish sauce

2 tablespoons sugar

2 tablespoons sweetened plum
   (maesil) extract, homemade
   (page 149) or store-bought

1 Peel and stem the onions. Cut two slits halfway through each onion, making sure not to cut all the way through. This is for the marinade to better permeate them. Place the onions in a container with a lid.

2 **Make the marinade:** In a blender, combine all the ingredients and blend until smooth.

3 Pour the marinade over the onions. Make sure the onions are fully submerged.

4 Cover and leave out at room temperature overnight, then place in the refrigerator and let the onions ferment for at least 1 to 2 weeks. They are ready when they are soft and translucent. Cut into quarters and serve.

MANUEL JANGAJJI
PICKLED WHOLE GARLIC CLOVES WITH GOCHUJANG
마늘장아찌

MAKES 2 CUPS

Jangajji is in the category of pickled banchan that are often aged for an extended period – in some cases more than six weeks. This is the definition of "set-it-and-forget-it" cooking, and jangajji is a cornerstone of Korea's long tradition of slow foods. Sweet and mild garlic jangajji is a particular favorite of grilled meat restaurants, and in Seoul, we encountered it at many of the barbecue spots we visited. In some cases, large cauldrons of the foundational Korean allium were offered to diners in a serve-yourself manner. But contrary to your possible snap judgment when presented with a bowl full of garlic cloves, these are far from the bracing "raw garlic" kick you might expect.

Garlic jangajji is prepared in two steps. First is the two-week soak in a water-vinegar solution. This step is essential to get rid of the crazy garlic punch. Next, the brined garlic is tossed in a marinade of gochujang, soy sauce, and sweetness. Once complete, this marinated pickle will keep in the fridge basically forever, and it can be pulled out as a banchan to pair with any grilled meat, bulgogi or kalbi, jokbal (long-simmered pork trotters), and any braises and stews. Jangajji can also be served as a snack with rice and kim. The same process can be used to pickle and season ramps, chiles, and pearl onions.

1 pound peeled garlic
    cloves, unbroken

BRINE

1 cup cider vinegar or rice vinegar

1 cup water

1 tablespoon kosher salt

MARINADE

½ cup gochujang

2 tablespoons coarsely ground
    gochugaru

2 tablespoons soy sauce

2 tablespoons mirin or soju

2 tablespoons rice syrup

1 tablespoon sweetened plum
    (maesil) or other fruit extract,
    homemade (page 149) or
    store-bought

1 **Brine the garlic:** Put the garlic cloves into a tall, airtight container. Add the vinegar, water, and salt and stir gently to dissolve the salt. Make sure the garlic is fully submerged in the vinegar-water solution.

2 Cover and refrigerate for 10 to 14 days. After this time, the garlic should be light brown and slightly translucent and taste less astringent.

3 **Make the marinade:** In a large bowl, combine all the ingredients and mix well.

4 Drain the brined garlic, add to the bowl of marinade, and mix well. Transfer to an airtight container.

5 Store in the refrigerator for about 1 month before eating. The longer the better, as the flavors develop more over time. The garlic banchan will keep in the refrigerator for months.

OI MUCHIM
SWEET-AND-SOUR 7UP PICKLED CUCUMBERS
오이무침

MAKES 3 CUPS

One day, after wrapping up a visit to Majang Meat Market, and with plastic bags stuffed with chadol and kalbi in hand, we found ourselves at Soot Bull Tak Tak, a great barbecue restaurant. Deuki did his thing, manning the grill, and we had the best time. After the meal was wrapped up, we noticed that, even while stuffed, we kept returning to the pickled cucumber banchan that had been attentively refilled several times. It wasn't the hard sour snap of, say, Katz's full sour pickles, or the lightly marinated (and oftentimes watery) seasoned cukes that are commonly served at Korean BBQs. This pickle was tart, slightly sweet, a little effervescent, and addictive. We inquired, and the server admitted that lemon-lime soda (Sprite, 7UP, whichever is your brand of choice) was used in the recipe. It's so good. Here's our version, which we think is the best banchan ever to serve with barbecue at home.

1 pound small Kirby cucumbers, sliced

2 garlic cloves, minced

½ red finger chile or other medium-hot chile (such as cayenne or serrano), minced

1 cup water

½ cup rice vinegar

⅓ cup sugar

4 teaspoons kosher salt

½ cup 7UP or Sprite

Sesame oil, for serving

1   Pack a clean, heatproof 1-quart container with the cucumbers, garlic, and chile.

2   In a small saucepan, combine the water, vinegar, sugar, and salt and bring to a boil over medium-high heat, stirring to dissolve the sugar and salt. Remove from the heat and pour the hot pickling liquid over the cucumbers. Top off with the 7UP. Stir gently along the sides to combine.

3   Let cool to room temperature, then cover and refrigerate ideally for a couple of hours. Serve the pickles cold with some of the liquid and a small drizzle of sesame oil stirred in. The pickles will keep in the refrigerator for up to 2 weeks.

DWAEJI KALBI
GRILLED SPICY PORK BABY BACK RIBS
돼지갈비

SERVES 4

In Korea, the smell of pork can be a turnoff to some diners, which is why pork is often slathered in a powerful sauce, typically built around gochujang. This gorgeous savory, fruit-based marinade, which we've been making for backyard barbecues for years, needs to flavor the ribs for at least four hours, but ideally the marinating ribs will hang out in the fridge overnight. And we say it now, and have said it before: There is no better party favor than bringing over a couple of freezer bags stuffed with marinated ribs. Throw them on the grill, and the backyard has been instantly transformed into your favorite Korean barbecue restaurant.

MARINADE

1 Gala or Fuji apple, peeled, cored, and roughly chopped

½ Asian pear, peeled and roughly chopped

½ white onion, roughly chopped

4 garlic cloves, roughly chopped

1 cup gochujang

¼ cup soy sauce

¼ cup rice syrup

2 tablespoons mirin

¼ cup finely ground gochugaru

2 tablespoons sugar

1 tablespoon ground black pepper

2 full racks of baby back ribs (5 to 7 pounds total), silver skin removed

Sesame seeds, for garnish

1 **Make the marinade:** In a food processor or blender, combine all the ingredients and process until smooth. It's best to prepare this marinade a day ahead and refrigerate it overnight to allow the flavors to mingle.

2 Cut the rib racks into individual ribs by slicing between the bones. Transfer the ribs to a large bowl or ziplock bag, pour the marinade over the ribs, and massage the marinade into the ribs for 30 seconds to coat them fully. Cover the bowl or seal the bag and marinate in the refrigerator for at least 4 hours and preferably 24 hours.

3 **To grill:** Prepare a charcoal or gas grill for direct cooking over medium heat. To check if it's ready, place your hand 6 inches above the grate; you should be able to withstand the heat for only about 5 seconds before pulling away. Remove the ribs from the marinade, shaking off any excess. Place the ribs on the grate and cook, flipping frequently, until well browned and cooked through, 15 to 20 minutes.

4 **To roast:** Preheat the oven to 350°F. Set a wire rack on a sheet pan and arrange the ribs in a single layer, not touching, on the rack. Roast until the meat is tender and cooked through, about 45 minutes.

5 Transfer the ribs to a platter and let rest for 5 minutes. Garnish with sesame seeds and serve.

POST-BARBECUE BOKKEUMBAP
볶음밥

SERVES 4 TO 6

It's the ultimate act of Korean hospitality. It's almost a Korean restaurant parlor trick, yet there's no fooling. The extra bokkeumbap course to close a feast is always a welcome surprise, especially when we experienced it at Mongtan in Seoul. The hiss of the barbecue grill has slowed down, and the meat coma has started to creep in. Yet there is always room for a final dish, right? A server arrives with a pot of steamed rice, an often mysterious sauce (usually red), and a game plan. The rice is pressed into the grill pan or cast-iron skillet, where it soaks up the meat residue left over after rounds and rounds of sizzling kalbi.

We wanted to adapt this concept for an at-home fried rice, and we think we've nailed it here. It's a great way to close your own Korean barbecue meal — and it's super easy to pull off. Just have some rice and sauce on hand and bring it to the table (if you are grilling tableside) or drop it into the cast-iron grill pan that is just sitting there with all that incredible flavor waiting to be activated.

SAUCE
¼ cup gochujang

2 tablespoons oyster sauce

1 tablespoon soy sauce

1 tablespoon mirin

2 teaspoons sesame oil

½ teaspoon sugar

RICE
4 cups cooked short- or medium-grain rice (preferably day old)

2 tablespoons neutral cooking oil

1 large onion, diced small

6 garlic cloves, minced

2 teaspoons gochugaru

Kosher salt and ground black pepper

½ cup fresh chive batons, in 2-inch lengths, or 3 scallions, green parts, sliced

1 **Make the sauce:** In a small bowl, combine all the ingredients and mix well. Set aside.

2 **Cook the rice:** Break up any clumps in the rice. Heat the oil in a large cast-iron or nonstick skillet over medium-high heat until it shimmers. Add the onion and cook, stirring often, until softened and browned, about 3 minutes. Add the garlic and gochugaru and stir until the mixture is very fragrant, about 30 seconds.

3 Lower the heat to medium, add the sauce, and stir for a few seconds. Add the rice and stir until fully combined. Cook, stirring occasionally, until the rice is dry and starting to toast, about 3 minutes. Season with salt and pepper. Transfer to a serving bowl and top with the chives.

4 This may be served as is, but if you're using a grill pan, enjoy this post-barbecue treat: Spread out the rice in the grill pan and place over medium heat. Press down on the rice, allowing it to brown and crisp and absorb all the flavor of the meat remnants and fat in the pan. Then scoop it out and place in a bowl, season with salt and pepper, top with the chives, and serve.

MU KIMCHI GRANITA
RADISH KIMCHI GRANITA
얼음 물김치

MAKES 1 CUP; SERVES 4 TO 8

We spotted many cool versions of frozen kimchi (a totally new idea in the past couple of years) in a few places around Korea, and we think one of the best applications is as a granita to serve alongside other banchan at the barbecue table or as a closing icy note to segue into dessert. When offered super cold, enjoyed in small spoonfuls served individually or communally, it's a refreshing play of textures with the crushed frozen kimchi brine and radish. This goes really well with Air Fryer Pork Belly (page 139), providing a nice hot-cold contrast.

½ cup brine from jar of radish kimchi (kkakdugi)

4 ounces Korean radish or daikon, peeled and cut into matchsticks (about 1 cup)

1 small garlic clove, minced

¼ teaspoon peeled, minced fresh ginger

2 teaspoons gochugaru

½ teaspoon kosher salt

½ teaspoon sugar

1   Pour the brine into an ice cube tray (it will not fill the entire tray) and freeze overnight.

2   In a small bowl, combine the radish, garlic, ginger, gochugaru, salt, and sugar and massage together until the radish is stained an orange red. Cover and refrigerate for at least 30 minutes.

3   Pop out the kimchi ice cubes into a food processor. Pulse a few times, then process to the texture of snow. Scrape into a medium bowl, immediately add the radish mixture, and mix together quickly as the granita will start to melt.

BIBIM NAENGMYEON
SPICY BUCKWHEAT NOODLES
비빔냉면

SERVES 4

At the end of a Korean barbecue feast, you are either a bibim naengmyeon (spicy, chewy cold noodles) person or a mul naengmyeon (tangy, brothy, colder noodles) person. But either way, chilled buckwheat noodles with kicks of acid are the finest beef digestive we know.

This recipe is all about bibim naengmyeon, which means it's all about spice. Ideally, make the sauce the day before. Time is an ingredient here, and it's best to let the gochujang, gochugaru, pineapple, apples, mirin, and other ingredients marry and mellow overnight. Then it's all about the assembly, which, for all styles of naengmyeon, is a matter of preference. Egg or no egg? Hot mustard or no hot mustard? Place all the accoutrements on the table and let your diners decide. As for the sauce, it will keep for a couple of weeks in the fridge, and any that's left over can be used as a great bibimbap sauce.

SAUCE

2 cups coarsely ground gochugaru

½ cup gochujang

1 small onion, roughly chopped

¼ cup peeled, coarsely chopped Gala apple

¼ cup canned crushed pineapple, drained

6 garlic cloves, coarsely chopped

½ cup soy sauce

½ cup rice syrup

½ cup cider vinegar or rice vinegar

¼ cup mirin or soju

¼ cup sweetened plum (maesil) or other fruit extract, homemade (page 149) or store-bought

¼ cup sesame oil

¼ cup Dashida beef stock base

2 tablespoons sugar

1 pound dried naengmyeon noodles

½ cup julienned English cucumber

¼ cup peeled, julienned Asian pear

Hot mustard, for serving

Rice vinegar, for serving

1   **Make the sauce:** In a medium bowl, combine the gochugaru and gochujang and set aside.

2   In a blender, combine the onion, apple, pineapple, garlic, soy sauce, rice syrup, vinegar, mirin, plum extract, oil, stock base, and sugar and blend until smooth.

3   Pour the contents of the blender into the gochugaru mixture and mix well. This is your sauce. It's best to make it a day ahead and refrigerate it in an airtight container to allow the flavors to develop.

4   Have ready a large bowl of ice water. Bring a large pot of water to a boil over high heat. Add the noodles and cook according to the package instructions. Drain well, then shock them in the ice water until chilled.

5   Using tongs, lift the noodles from the ice water and divide equally among four bowls. Top each bowl with the cucumber and pear, dividing them evenly, and ¼ cup of the sauce. Serve with mustard and vinegar.

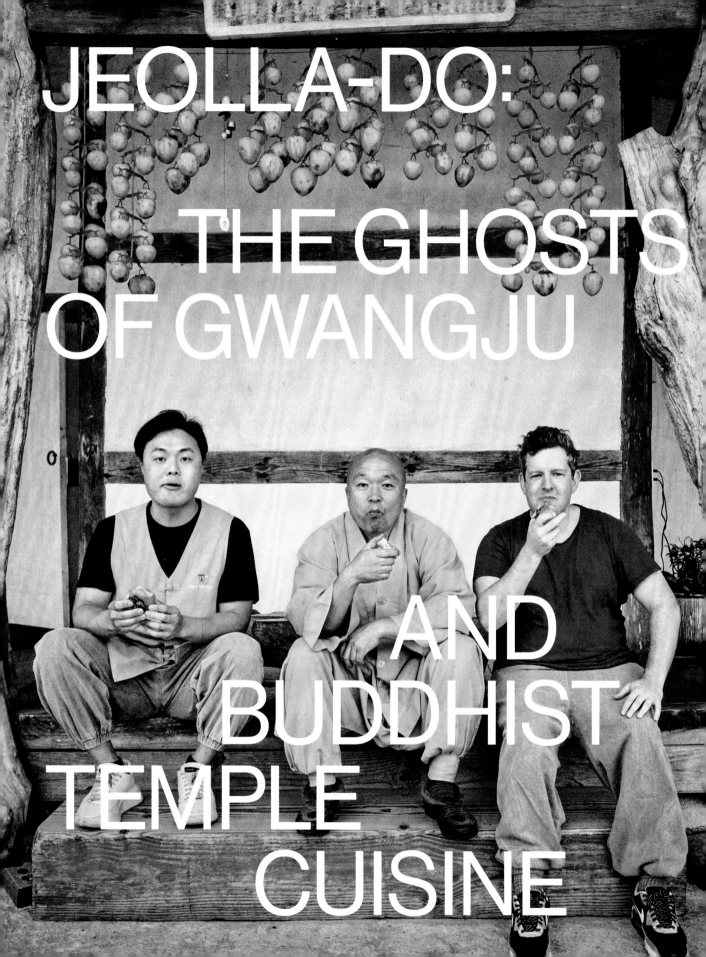

JEOLLA-DO: THE GHOSTS OF GWANGJU AND BUDDHIST TEMPLE CUISINE

Located on the southwestern shin of the Korean peninsula, Jeolla-do is widely considered to be home to Korea's best food, be it fermented jangs, pasture-raised beef, or the elaborate banchan that are served with many meals. The country's biggest kimchi festival, started in 1994, is held in Gwangju, the region's largest city, and a number of Buddhist monasteries in the area open their doors to tourists through organized temple stays. These temples are fostering a new chapter in plant-based cooking in Korea.

In this section, we approach that temple cuisine from many angles, with recipes for plant-based doenjang jjigae, broccoli salad with ssamjang mayo, and a mille-feuille–inspired jjigae of cabbage and mushrooms. We were able to spend time in a couple of temple kitchens and found that the food, which boasts a long tradition, was just beginning to gain popularity beyond the monastery walls when it had its star turn on Netflix's *Chef's Table* in 2017.

We also spent time in Gwangju and came to understand how Korea's sixth-largest city has a dark history—one that is widely known in Korea but hardly anywhere else. We tell that story while offering up recipes for what we agree is if not the best food region in Korea (what an impossible call that is!) then certainly an underreported one.

Korean Temple Food: After the Netflix Cameras Went Home

The chewing sounds are deafening—at least relative to the calm outside the sixth-century Buddhist monastery Hwaeomsa, located in the foothills of Jirisan mountain in Korea's Jeolla Province, a four-hour drive south of Seoul. In the fall of 2021, we traveled to Hwaeomsa to get a sense of how Korea's ancient temple cuisine is prepared. It's an honest, spiritual kind of cooking that is a daily practice in a temple of more than thirty monks and nuns—and the occasional Korean visitor looking to unplug from the daily grind.

And so we stood in the corner of a spotless dining hall at 5:10 a.m. and watched, and listened to, the monks eat breakfast: a well-considered buffet-style spread of deep flavor and tongue-snapping fermentation that included many Korean national dishes prepared without any animal products and certain astringent flavors. A temple kitchen essentially bans the use of five hot and overpowering vegetables (onions, garlic, scallions, chives, and leeks). Called oshinchae, they are perceived to hinder the concentration needed for spiritual practice. And in accordance, we find allium-free versions of doenjang jjigae (soybean paste stew), marinated dubu (tofu), and baechu (napa cabbage) kimchi. Their deep flavors showed this to be far from a cuisine whose main feature is what it lacks.

This isn't the Korean monk-chef cooking made famous on Netflix's highly styled *Chef's Table* a number of years back. There's no concerto of Vivaldi violins to be found or, until our arrival, Western media dropping in for an interview. Instead, through our visits to Hwaeomsa and other temples around Seoul, we found workaday temple food— and passionate, if anonymous to Western readers, chefs preparing it—that had the innate beauty and creativity that was made famous on television. There are no celebrity-chef pilgrimages to this temple tucked into a corner of Jirisan. Yet the food we found being prepared in the cafeteria-style kitchen was honest and, most important, stunningly delicious. The bowl of plant-based jjigae, shaped with a stock of kim (seaweed), foraged shiitake mushrooms, daikon, and the chef's stash of homemade doenjang (fermented bean paste), was one of the most satisfying bowls of soup we've ever tasted.

When *Chef's Table* dropped the first episode of its third season in February 2017—a season featuring well-known American chefs Ivan Orkin and Nancy Silverton—relatively little was known outside Korea about the cuisine of Korean Buddhism, a practice first introduced seventeen hundred years ago. Two years prior, journalist Jeff Gordinier had written about monk-chef Jeong Kwan and her culinary tutelage of chef (and practicing Buddhist) Eric Ripert, of Michelin three-starred Le Bernardin, in the *New York Times Magazine*. But it was the global reach of Netflix, as well as the visionary approach to food documentary filmmaking of *Chef's Table*, that had the world mesmerized. "I make food as a meditation," Kwan says at the close of the episode. "I am living my life as a monk with a blissful mind and freedom."

The episode happened to premiere during a time of rising mainstream interest in meditation and mindfulness along with plant-based eating, and it was followed by visits to Kwan's temple from globally lauded chefs, including Noma's René Redzepi and Maison Aribert's Christophe Aribert, and to extended residencies by well-regarded Korean chefs Mingoo Kang (see page 48) of Mingles in Seoul and Kwang Uh, formerly of Baroo in Los Angeles and currently of Shiku in the city's Grand Central Market.

"The spirit of temple food that monk Jeong Kwan mentioned is respect and gratitude for all life, and all life is connected," observes Younglim Kim, a team leader at the Cultural Corps of Korean Buddhism. "All the monks and believers in Korean Buddhism think [about that] the same way," she adds. "However, the food culture varies, and the temple food of Jeong Kwan does not apply equally to other temples or other regions." Kim likens the varying styles of temple cuisine to that of kimchi, noting that the food prepared by monks and nuns in northern Gangwon may differ significantly from that of the Busan region in the peninsula's southeast and of the Jeolla region in the southwest, where we are watching the nun-chef Kyungjin Lee prepare morning jjigae for residents and guests.

Kim, who leads the Buddhist Monastic Cuisine program in the Cultural Corps, views the diversity of temple cuisine as a gateway for outsiders to learn about Korean heritage, partake in Buddhist traditions, and eat rustic cooking that eschews the stereotype of Korean food as exclusively a barbecue and bibimbap affair. In pre-pandemic 2019, more than 460,000 Koreans and 70,000 foreigners partook in a temple stay program, and the number is expected to grow significantly as the world continues to embrace Korean food and culture.

For our second temple visit, our group traveled north of Seoul to Jinkwansa Temple, tucked at the edge of the hilly Bukhansan National Park, which, on this cloudless day, had autumn's electric leaf display cranked up to eleven. While Hwaeomsa had the feeling of a summer camp, Jinkwansa was slicker and more polished (Jill Biden visited in 2015) and included a gift shop selling books and prayer beads, manicured vegetable gardens, and a hospitable and chatty monk named Sun Woo. (Ever wonder how a screening of *Parasite* would play to a crowd of monastic students? Sun Woo has a story.)

Jinkwansa is also one of the few all-female monasteries in Korea, and on the morning of our arrival, our group is led to meet with chief monk Gye Ho. She will first talk about the rise of temple cuisine in Korea and then make some fresh dubu (tofu) using the most traditional methods, which involve soaked soybeans, a large grinder called a maet dol, and Gye Ho's smiling directions.

With our group seated in a sunny room styled with striking blond woods, Gye Ho espouses the link between food and religion. "It's like a medicine for the human body," she says through a translator. Gye Ho, now in her seventies, became a nun at age nineteen and channeled a love of cooking into her practice, studying under several master monks. "Cooking is the extension of my practice. Feeding the body is the same as feeding the mind."

During our time in Korea over the past decade, we've observed temple cuisine in many forms. Matt was once served a small nest of sautéed burdock root sweetened with ganjang (soy sauce) and orchard fruits as part of a multicourse tasting worthy of high critical praise. We've had a messy bowl of rice porridge (juk) streaked with sesame oil for breakfast, and even tasted Jeong Kwan's cooking at the ultra-rarified Le Bernardin in New York, during a special guest luncheon hosted by Ripert.

On this recent visit, we sampled chef Kyungjin Lee's plant-based baechu (napa cabbage) kimchi, which is typically seasoned with fish sauce or shrimp paste, two items banned from this kitchen. It was sweet and fresh, only marinated for a day, and it changed the way we have thought about the so-called vegan kimchi that has become so popular in the United States.

"Over seventeen hundred years have passed since Buddhism was introduced to Korea," Younglim Kim reminds us. "And since recipes are being passed down, Jeong Kwan cannot represent them all." Nor should we expect the full story of any cuisine or culture from a single chef. Jeong Kwan—and her skilled marketing and publicity team—deserve credit for evangelizing temple cuisine (and naturally the religion, too) through media and events around the world. The results have been spectacular in raising awareness for Korean food and culture writ large, but this Buddhist temple cuisine story is most certainly more than what you see on television. The future is bright and full of exciting recipes—some of which we've developed versions of here.

ALL-PURPOSE MUSHROOM STOCK

버섯 육수

MAKES 4 QUARTS

This stock was a staple in the kitchen when we visited the sixth-century Buddhist monastery Hwaeomsa in Jeolla Province. The combination of mushrooms and mushroom powder is a potent base for the plant-based cooking we have enjoyed throughout Korea. Steeping the kombu, the final step, adds a rich layer to this utility stock we use for many of our plant-based jjigaes and tangs.

4 quarts water

2-inch knob fresh ginger, peeled and sliced

1 tablespoon mushroom powder

2 cups fresh or 1 cup dried shiitake mushrooms

2 cups thickly sliced Korean radish or daikon

One 6-inch square kombu (dashima)

1   In a large pot, combine the water, ginger, mushroom powder, mushrooms, and radish and bring to a boil over high heat. Lower the heat to medium-high heat and cook until the radish is translucent.

2   Remove from the heat, add the kombu, and steep for 30 minutes.

3   Strain the stock through a fine-mesh sieve and use immediately or reserve for future use. It will keep in one or more airtight containers in the refrigerator for up to 1 week or in the freezer for up to 6 months. For ease of use, freeze some of the stock in ice-cube trays.

BROCCOLI SALAD WITH SSAMJANG MAYO

쌈장 마요네즈 브로콜리 샐러드

SERVES 4

When we visited the cooks at the Hwaeomsa Buddhist monastery, we found vegetables everywhere – vegetables from the garden, vegetables from the root cellar, vegetables dried and reconstituted in the form of a broth. Broccoli was one of these constant vegetables, and this salad really surprised us. We loved the ssamjang mayo that was dolloped atop the blanched florets. We didn't ask if the mayo was vegan, but we assume it was, so feel free to use your favorite vegan brand (we call for the egg-based, extremely delicious, and MSG-packed Kewpie brand). Ssamjang is the condiment that is a constant at all KBBQ tables. But when it's transformed into a mayo, it opens it up to so many other possibilities, including being slathered on a burger or sandwich, set up with a vegetable tray, or dolloped atop blanched broccoli florets as we do here. We love this recipe, and we can't stop making this salad when company shows up.

2 heads broccoli

Kosher salt

1 cup Kewpie brand mayonnaise

2 tablespoons doenjang

1 tablespoon gochujang

1 teaspoon sesame oil

1 Cut the broccoli into bite-size florets. (Or buy a bag or two of prepared florets and save yourself the time.)

2 Bring a large pot of well-salted water to a boil. Drop in the broccoli florets and cook for 1 minute—no longer! Drain and rinse with cold running water for a minute or two. This will stop the cooking process and ensure the broccoli remains a verdant green. Dry the broccoli completely. This is important, as you do not want residual water mixing with the salad dressing.

3 To make the dressing, in a small bowl, whisk together the mayonnaise, doenjang, gochujang, and oil.

4 Top the broccoli with the dressing. If you want to do as the temple cooks do, dollop a small spoonful atop each floret to form a pattern.

DOTORIMUK BAP
ACORN JELLY "NOODLES" WITH RICE
도토리묵밥

SERVES 4 TO 6

This refreshing plant-based soup re-creates the satisfaction of "noodles" using acorn flour, which can be found at all Asian grocery stores or ordered online. The dotorimuk (acorn jelly) is really all about its bouncy and firm texture, which Koreans like. This bowl of "noodles" is served with fresh kimchi, cucumbers, seaweed, and a refreshing broth that works equally well hot or cold. Note this recipe makes a lot of acorn jelly, but it will keep well for a week in the fridge. Use it as a cold noodle substitute or as a banchan for your Korean lunch or dinner.

ACORN JELLY

12 cups water

2 cups acorn flour

1 tablespoon kosher salt

2 tablespoons sesame oil

MUSHROOM BROTH

8 cups All-Purpose Mushroom Stock (page 117), at room temperature if serving the dish cold

3 tablespoons soy sauce

1 tablespoon kosher salt

2 cups drained, sliced fresh napa kimchi

2 tablespoons sesame oil

1 tablespoon sugar

2 cups cooked short-grain rice, at room temperature

1 Kirby cucumber, peeled and sliced

8 perilla leaves, thinly sliced

Four to six 6-inch square sheets roasted and seasoned nori seaweed (kim)

Sesame seeds

1   **Make the acorn jelly:** In a large pot, bring 8 cups of the water to a boil.

2   While the water is heating, in a medium bowl, whisk together the flour and the remaining 4 cups water until smooth.

3   When the water is boiling, pour in the flour mixture, stir well, lower the heat to medium, and cook, stirring frequently, until the mixture is thick and starchy, 20 to 25 minutes. Stir in the salt and sesame oil and remove from the heat.

4   Oil the bottom and sides of a 9 by 13-inch baking pan with sesame oil. Pour the flour mixture into the prepared pan and let sit at room temperature for 12 hours. The acorn jelly should be moist and hardened like a firm Jell-O.

5   **Make the mushroom broth:** Season the stock with the soy sauce and salt. If you want to serve the broth hot, pour it into a medium pot and warm it over medium heat until piping hot.

6   In a small bowl, season the kimchi with the oil and sugar, mixing well.

7   To assemble the dish, divide the rice among four to six bowls. Slice about one-third of the acorn jelly into thin "noodles" and add to the bowls, dividing them evenly. (Refrigerate the remainder in an airtight container for future use.) Garnish with the cucumber, perilla, seasoned kimchi, seaweed, and sesame seeds.

8   Pour the mushroom broth into the bowls and serve.

The Ghosts of 5·18: Never Forget the 1980 Gwangju Uprising

There are ghosts in Gwangju, the historically and culturally significant city of 1.5 million residents located in the heart of the agricultural Jeolla-do region. Known for its superior kimchi and jangs as well as its thriving arts scene, this vibrant city was also the site of a dark moment in Korean history.

From May 18 to May 27, 1980, violence rocked the city as a peaceful demonstration against the authoritarian military leader Chun Doo-hwan escalated into bloodshed when fully outfitted Korean military forces advanced against the lightly armed students and local residents. The fighting was fierce, with the overmatched demonstrators fighting bravely against tanks and machine guns. Death came quickly and violently for many, and while the official government death toll is documented as 170, it is widely accepted that between 1,000 and 2,300 residents perished—with some bodies being thrown into unmarked graves by government forces in a clear cover-up.

In 1997, a national cemetery and a day of commemoration on May 18 were established, and the episode is now widely known as 5·18. The uprising has been covered extensively in both literature and film. Han Kang's 2014 novel *Human Acts* tackles 5·18 through the story of a boy murdered by government troops and how his life (and spirit) travels through to the present time. It demonstrates how the bloody crackdown still strikes a raw nerve with many Koreans.

In November 2021, we visited the 5·18 Memorial Park and Memorial Hall. Lined neatly on a slight slope are, as of this writing, 482 graves of those who died in 1980 and those who participated. Within the hall are artifacts from the siege. Bloodstained uniforms and pieces of cement are on display to remind visitors of the many atrocities and acts of heroism that occurred during those ten days in May more than four decades ago.

TEMPLE CABBAGE-PERSIMMON KIMCHI
사찰 감김치

SERVES 4

We wanted to land on a plant-based napa cabbage kimchi that wasn't the typical vegan kimchi fare, and all it took was looking around the grounds of the Hwaeomsa monastery. The trees were bursting with bright orange persimmons, a difficult-to-characterize fruit that could be described as a slightly sweeter tomato. We found the chefs at Hwaeomsa using persimmons in many ways, including as a base for an autumn cabbage kimchi. This relatively fast kimchi can be eaten right away or aged for months. It's less biting than the baby shrimp or fish sauce–based versions some people are accustomed to, but it's certainly just as enjoyable.

CABBAGE

5 cups water

½ cup kosher salt

2 medium or large heads napa cabbage

GOCHUGARU MIXTURE

3 ripe Hachiya persimmons, peeled, seeded, and mashed

1-inch knob fresh ginger, peeled and minced

½ cup coarsely ground gochugaru

3 tablespoons soy sauce

½ cup kosher salt

1 Korean radish or daikon, peeled and julienned

1 medium carrot, peeled and julienned

RICE PORRIDGE

3 cups water

¼ cup glutinous rice

Three 3-inch squares kombu (dashima)

1   **Brine the cabbage:** In a bowl or tub large enough to hold the cabbages, whisk together the water and salt until the salt dissolves.

2   Split the cabbage heads lengthwise into quarters. Immerse the cabbages in the brine and leave for 4 hours. Then remove from the brine, rinse under cold running water, drain well, and set aside. Discard the brine.

3   **Make the gochugaru mixture:** In a large bowl, combine all the ingredients and mix well.

4   **Make the rice porridge:** In a small saucepan, combine the water, rice, and kombu and bring to a boil over medium-high heat. Turn down the heat to medium and simmer, stirring frequently, until the mixture has reduced and thickened to a porridge consistency, 20 to 30 minutes. Remove from the heat and let cool.

5   When the porridge is cool, add it to the gochugaru mixture and mix well.

6   Glove up and thoroughly coat each cabbage quarter with the mixture. Put the coated cabbage in a lidded container for storage. Let sit at room temperature for 24 hours, then place in the refrigerator for 2 weeks before serving. This is best eaten within a month, but it will keep refrigerated for much longer.

MILLE-FEUILLE CABBAGE AND MUSHROOM JJIGAE
밀푀유 양배추버섯찌개

SERVES 4

The mille-feuille is a famously layered and creamy French pastry, sometimes called the Napoleon, but in recent years, it's been flipped to the savory side of the coin, particularly in Japan, where it's been transformed into a nabe (hot pot). When we were visiting the Buddhist temples in and around Jeolla-do and Seoul, we all got to talking: Could a plant-based jjigae be channeled into a Korean-style mille-feuille? After lots of testing, the answer is yes, yes, yes!

Here classic jjigae seasoning is layered between cabbage and mushrooms. There is nothing humble – a word often associated with Korean temple cuisine – about this stunning plant-based main dish incorporating napa cabbage, trumpet mushrooms, perilla leaves, and Korean radish.

1 head napa cabbage (about 3 pounds), leaves separated

20 perilla leaves

4 cups black trumpet mushrooms, halved lengthwise

1 large Korean radish or daikon, peeled and cut into small cubes

2 cups bean sprouts

One 14-ounce package soft tofu, drained and cut into medium cubes

8 cups All-Purpose Mushroom Stock (page 117)

SEASONING

¼ cup doenjang

2 tablespoons gochujang

1 tablespoon sugar

1 tablespoon soy sauce

2 teaspoons peeled, minced fresh ginger

1 teaspoon gochugaru

1 tablespoon kosher salt or mushroom powder

1   To create the mille-feuille pattern, start with a cabbage leaf, top with two perilla leaves side by side, and then add a sprinkling of mushrooms to form a layer. Repeat twice, to create three layers stacked on top of one another. Place a cabbage leaf on top of the stack, then cut the stack lengthwise into thirds. Repeat the stacking with the remaining cabbage, perilla, and mushrooms and then cut as above.

2   **Make the seasoning:** In a small bowl, combine all the ingredients and mix well. Transfer the seasoning to the bottom of a large serving pot. A cast-iron Dutch oven works great here. Cover with the radish, bean sprouts, and tofu.

3   Working from the rim of the pot toward the center, neatly place the cabbage-stack pieces, cut side up so the cross section of the mille-feuille is visible, on top of the tofu bed. They should be packed tightly together.

4   Pour the stock over everything, place on the stove top, and bring to a boil over high heat. Then drop the heat to medium, cover, and simmer until the cabbage is soft and tender, about 10 minutes. Serve immediately.

TEMPLE DUBU JORIM
SOY SAUCE–MARINATED TOFU
사찰 두부조림

SERVES 4

Watching the temple cooks at the Hwaeomsa monastery patiently slice and stack chunks of tofu at 5:00 a.m. was something we'll never forget. As they readied the morning meal for the quiet, hungry monks, we stood on the sidelines and watched in our own sleepy silence. This is one of the dishes that stuck with us the most: a very lightly braised tofu served cold with bowls of rice and seasoned vegetables. While nothing beats fresh tofu (check your local bodega or market for it), the packaged stuff works pretty well too. After frying the tofu to a pleasant shade of golden brown, we add the flavorful marinade that braises and bubbles with the bean curd until it reaches a nice caramelized state.

MARINADE

1 apple, peeled and grated
2 tablespoons soy sauce
2 tablespoons water
1 tablespoon sesame oil
1 tablespoon rice syrup
1 tablespoon sugar
1 teaspoon gochugaru
2 teaspoons mushroom powder

2 tablespoons neutral cooking oil
One 18-ounce package firm tofu, drained and cut into 8 equal slabs

1   **Make the marinade:** In a small bowl, combine all the ingredients and mix well.

2   In a large skillet, heat the neutral oil over medium-high heat until it shimmers. Add the tofu and cook, turning the slabs frequently to prevent burning, until golden brown on both sides, 4 to 6 minutes.

3   Pour in the marinade, raise the heat to high, and cook, turning the tofu often, until it is well coated and the marinade has reduced by half.

4   Remove from the heat and let cool. Slice the tofu on the diagonal and serve.

JEJU-DO: AN ISLAND OF PORK AND TANGERINES

Jeju Island is sometimes called the Hawaii of Korea, and the valid observation points to the wealth of natural resources, striking vistas, and ancestral foodways that characterize this island fifty miles off the Korean mainland. Jeju is volcanic, and temperate, and attracts honeymooners from all around Asia, with an economy built around tourism. Though, to be fair, you will find more tangerines than pineapples there.

For years, plenty of friends—and many chefs and food folks—have emphatically recommended a visit to Jeju, and we were able to spend a couple of fall days driving and eating all around the island. We were struck by its remoteness, despite being an hour's flight from Seoul, and how the crashing sea leads to mountain ranges, including Korea's tallest peak, Mount Hallasan. Our focus was on the food, and we sampled the island's legendary heritage breed of black pigs, used for a gamier and incredibly flavorful style of barbecue. We also ate horse in a couple of preparations: one dish was yukhwe (raw meat) served with sesame oil and another one braised the meat in a simple soy sauce–based jjim. And around every corner, we found tangerines for sale. When this prized Korean citrus is in season in late fall and early winter, it is sold all over Asia.

But you primarily come to Jeju for the seafood, and Jeju seafood is intrinsically connected to the haenyeo, or female divers, whose grueling work demands both great skill and tremendous courage. Divers regularly plunge to depths of nearly one hundred feet with no breathing equipment in search of conch, abalone, octopus, and more. This dangerous work by a strictly female population has been woven into the lore of Jeju, and today it has come to symbolize female empowerment through its depiction in books and films.

Our journey around the island also had us eating many bowls of gogi guksu (literally, "meat noodles"), a hearty noodle dish found much less frequently on the Korean mainland and in the United States. Jeju is an island that offers a multitude of experiences, and through the brief time we spent visiting—and the much longer time we spent researching—we hope this short section gives you a taste of some of the recipes and stories of the island.

HWEDUBAP WITH YUJA CHOJANG
RAW FISH AND RICE SAUCE
회덮밥과 유자초장

SERVES 4

Koreans covet the freshest seafood humanly possible, so fresh that there's a long tradition of Korean fish-tank restaurants that specialize in saengseon-hwe. At these restaurants, which are found throughout Korea and in Koreatowns around the United States, diners place their order and the chefs go out back to rows and rows of tanks, where they pull the fish out alive, butcher them quickly, and serve them before the first round of soju has been finished. Unlike the raw fish served in a Japanese style, where it is aged for anywhere from a few days to a few weeks, hwe is a bit tougher; as with all freshly killed meat, rigor mortis soon sets in. For Koreans, the chewiness is all part of the deal. And instead of dipping the pieces of snapper or halibut in soy sauce, Koreans prefer a sweet and tangy condiment called chojang, a combination of rice vinegar, gochujang, and pineapple juice. At the Dongmun Market in Jeju City, we found raw mackerel, abalone, and sea bass served alongside red squeeze bottles of chojang.

This is our version of chojang, which we make a little sweeter to resemble the bibimbap sauce that you've likely poured over a stone or steel bowl of rice in the past. The key ingredient is the Korean honey citron concentrate called yuja cheong, which is most commonly used as the base of a tea (yuja cha).

YUJA CHOJANG

1 cup gochujang
¾ cup yuja cha (honey citron tea)
¼ cup rice vinegar or cider vinegar
¼ cup sugar
¼ cup soy sauce
2 tablespoons sesame oil
2 tablespoons sesame seeds
2 garlic cloves, minced

HWEDUBAP

½ small white onion
1 large carrot
1 English cucumber
1 small-to-medium head red leaf or romaine lettuce
6 perilla leaves
8 ounces sushi-grade salmon
8 ounces sushi-grade tuna
2 cups cooked short-grain rice, warm (not steaming hot)
½ cup masago or tobiko (fish roe)
Eight 4-inch squares roasted nori seaweed (kim), for garnish
2 teaspoons sesame seeds, for garnish
½ cup yuja chojang
1 lemon, quartered

1 **Make the chojang:** In a small bowl, whisk together all the ingredients. Cover and refrigerate overnight to allow the flavors to meld before serving. You will have about 3 cups sauce. Set aside ½ cup for the hwedubap. The remainder will keep in an airtight container or your own red squeeze bottle in the refrigerator for several weeks.

2 **Make the hwedubap:** Using a mandoline or a sharp knife, slice the onion paper-thin. Peel the carrot, then cut into julienne. Soak the onion and carrot in a small bowl of ice water so they remain fresh and crisp. Peel the cucumber, halve lengthwise, and cut the halves crosswise into half-moons. Roughly chop the lettuce and perilla leaves. Using scissors, cut the seaweed into thin strips. Set all the vegetables aside.

3 Have ready a chilled plate. Using a very sharp knife, slice the salmon and tuna across the grain into ¼-inch-thick slices and place on the chilled plate.

4 Divide the rice among four bowls. Add the cucumber, lettuce, and perilla. Remove the onion and carrot from the ice bath, shake them dry, and add them to the bowls. Arrange the fish and masago in the center of each bowl and garnish with seaweed and sesame seeds. Drizzle about 2 tablespoons of the chojang atop each bowl. (You will have some left that you might want to add later.) Serve the assembled bowls with the lemon wedges and invite diners to mix everything together.

JEJU GOGI GUKSU
JEJU-STYLE PORK AND NOODLES
제주 고기국수

SERVES 4

A Jeju Island specialty, gogi guksu offers one of the most pork-forward broths you will find in Korean cooking, closer to the rich, almost creamy bone broth of Japanese tonkotsu ramen than any of the classic Korean tangs and jjigaes. The mild broth is seasoned with a scoop of a crimson, spicy seasoning (a marriage of gochugaru, soy sauce, mirin, and alliums). This broth recipe is a simplified version that skips hard-to-find pork bones and overnight cooking.

1   Season the pork well all over with salt. Heat a Dutch oven or other large, heavy pot over medium heat until hot. Add the pork, skin side down, to the dry pot and sear, turning once, until evenly browned on both sides, 4 to 5 minutes on each side. Transfer the pork to a plate and set aside.

2   **Make the broth:** In the same pot, combine the water, doenjang, fish sauce, peppercorns, onion, garlic, and ginger over medium heat and simmer, stirring to dislodge all the browned bits (the fond) from the pot bottom.

3   Return the pork to the pot, raise the heat to high, bring to a boil, and then drop the temperature to medium and simmer, uncovered, for 1 hour, skimming off any fat and impurities from the surface periodically. The pork will be chewy but tender enough to slice. It should not be soft and falling apart.

4   **Make the seasoning:** While the pork and broth simmer, in a small bowl, combine all the ingredients, mix well, and set aside.

5   When the broth and pork are ready, transfer the pork to a cutting board and let cool. Strain the broth through a fine-mesh sieve into a clean medium saucepan. Add the beef broth to the strained broth and set aside. Once the pork has cooled, thinly slice against the grain.

6   Bring a large pot of water to a boil. Add the noodles and cook according to the package instructions. Drain and shock under cold running water.

7   To assemble, heat the broth to a simmer. Divide the noodles among four bowls and add 1 tablespoon of the seasoning to each bowl. Pour the hot broth on top, dividing it evenly. Garnish with the pork slices and scallions and serve immediately with the remaining seasoning on the side.

2 pounds skin-on pork belly or pork shoulder, in one piece

Kosher salt

1 pound dried thin somen or other wheat noodles

Sliced scallions, white and green parts, for garnish

BROTH

8 cups water

3 tablespoons doenjang

1 tablespoon fish sauce

10 whole black peppercorns

1 white onion, halved

3 garlic cloves, crushed

2-inch knob fresh ginger, peeled and smashed

4 cups beef broth

SEASONING

2 tablespoons minced scallions, white part only

2 garlic cloves, minced

1 tablespoon fish sauce

1 tablespoon mirin

1 tablespoon gochugaru

1 tablespoon soy sauce

½ teaspoon ground black pepper

JEJU WHOLE FRIED SMASHED ROCKFISH
제주 우럭탕수

SERVES 4

One afternoon on the eastern coast of Jeju Island, we found ourselves being treated to lunch in a quiet beachside restaurant run by a husband-and-wife team. After we asked politely for a look at the kitchen, the chef-owner obliged, and we were soon staring at a half dozen whole fried rockfish sitting in a basket awaiting their fate. And what a fate it was, as we discovered a few moments later when the fish were ladled with a sticky, fiery sauce close to the classic sticky sweet and slightly spicy Korean fried chicken yangnyeom sauce and brought tableside. There was a brief pause for whole fish photos, and then the chef, with a shrug, put on some plastic gloves and began to smash, smash, smash, breaking the fish into bite-size pieces – each piece with a little bit of fried skin, a little bit of sauce, and a little bit of perfectly cooked meat. "What a brilliant way to do whole fish," we said to each other instantly, and here we are with the recipe.

Rockfish is a great choice for a whole fried fish. Many fish are called rockfish, but in general, you are looking at a mild-flavored white fish similar to grouper, halibut, and even cod. Sea bass will work brilliantly too. Make sure to ask your fishmonger to clean the fish, and before frying it, you should score it all over. You can ask the fishmonger to do this as well. Be sure to mention you will be frying it whole and then smashing it. TMI? Not really.

Neutral cooking oil, for deep-frying and sautéing

½ cup all-purpose flour

½ cup potato starch

One 2- to 3-pound whole rockfish, cleaned and scored on both sides

1 small onion, diced small

1 Korean squash (aehobak) or zucchini, diced small

1 red or yellow bell pepper, seeded and diced small

1 carrot, peeled and diced small

½ cup ketchup

½ cup gochujang

3 tablespoons rice syrup

2 tablespoons sugar

2 tablespoons minced garlic

½ cup chicken stock

3 scallions, green part only, sliced, for garnish

2 tablespoons or more sesame seeds, for garnish

1   Pour the oil to a depth of 2 inches into a cast-iron Dutch oven or other heavy pot large enough to hold the whole fish and heat over medium-high heat to 350°F.

2   While the oil is heating, whisk the flour and potato starch on a large, shallow plate. Dredge the fish in the mixture, coating it evenly and tapping off the excess.

3   When the oil is ready, carefully lower the fish into the hot oil and fry until the outside is golden brown and the inside is cooked, 18 to 20 minutes. Using tongs, transfer the fish to a plate.

4   Meanwhile, in a medium sauté pan, heat 3 tablespoons oil over medium-high until it shimmers. Add the onion, squash, bell pepper, and carrot and sauté until soft, 7 to 9 minutes. Add the ketchup, gochujang, rice syrup, sugar, garlic, and stock, stir well, raise the heat to high, and cook, stirring occasionally, until the sauce reduces slightly, about 10 minutes.

5   When the sauce is ready, pour it over the fish and garnish with scallions and sesame seeds.

6   Carry the fish to the table and, using rubber or disposable gloves, smash it tableside into large bite-size pieces, making sure the sauce is incorporated completely. Invite your guests to eat with their hands, removing the bones with their fingers or teeth.

CRISPY AIR FRYER PORK BELLY
삼겹살구이

SERVES 4 TO 6

This is our tribute to the famed black pig of Jeju. When well prepared, it takes on a rich porky flavor similar to that of such heritage breeds as Berkshire and Duroc. This is also a tribute to a piece of kitchen equipment that has taken the universe by storm, the air fryer. But a convection oven using the same temperatures as the air fryer will also achieve the crispy skin that defines the Jeju pork experience.

2 pounds skin-on pork belly

2 teaspoons kosher salt

½ teaspoon ground black pepper

4 teaspoons mirin

2 teaspoons doenjang

1-inch knob fresh ginger, peeled and grated

Distilled white vinegar, for brushing

Meljeot, for serving (recipe follows)

1 Prick the skin of the pork belly all over with a skewer, the tip of a paring knife, or a meat tenderizer. Poke lots of little holes close together to get crisp, bubbly skin. Be careful not to pierce the flesh, which could inhibit the crisping process.

2 If you have a whole slab or large pieces, cut the pork belly into roughly 3-inch-wide strips. (They will be easier to slice later.) Flip the strips meat side up. Rub the meat all over with 1½ teaspoons of the salt and the pepper. In a small bowl, stir together the mirin, doenjang, and ginger, mixing well. Brush the mixture over every bit of the meat, avoiding the skin.

3 Place each pork belly strip skin side up on its own square of aluminum foil (or you can put two similar-size pieces together). Wrap and fold the foil to make a tray that fits snugly against the sides of the pork belly, exposing just the top and sides of the skin.

4 Rub off any traces of the mirin mixture from the skin and blot the skin dry. Rub the remaining ½ teaspoon salt all over the skin. Refrigerate the pork belly strips uncovered in their foil trays overnight to dry the skin further. Periodically blot the skin if you see moisture collecting on the surface.

5 The next day, preheat the air fryer to 300°F. Just before cooking, blot the skin dry again and brush it with vinegar. Put the trays of pork belly in the air fryer and cook for 30 minutes. The pork will be browned, with some bubbles starting to appear on the skin.

6 Raise the temperature to 400°F and cook the pork belly until the skin is fully puffed and bubbly, 8 to 10 minutes. Let rest on a cutting board for 5 minutes, then slice and serve with the meljeot.

Meljeot
Anchovy Dipping Sauce
멜젓

On Jeju, the prized black pig barbecue is grilled over a live fire and dipped in meljeot, an über-salty and slightly spicy sauce that is a long-honored tradition for those vacationing on the island. This is a great sauce to make for any barbecue occasion, served alongside ssamjang (page 91).

In a small saucepan, whisk together all the ingredients and bring to a boil over medium heat. Serve warm with the pork belly or other Korean barbecue.

1 cup soju

3 tablespoons fish sauce

1 tablespoon minced garlic

2 tablespoons coarsely ground gochugaru

¼ onion, sliced

1 Korean green chile, sliced

3 garlic cloves, sliced

TANGERINE SALAD WITH CHILE
귤 샐러드

SERVES 4 TO 6

On Jeju Island, we kept seeing tangerines everywhere. Sold out of the back of vans. Neatly stacked in bowls at breakfast. Juiced with high-tech machinery at markets. On hats. (So many hats!) Tangerines are a big industry in Jeju, and the perfect way to eat them is in a salad that marries the flesh of in-season citrus with the heat of both fresh and dried chiles. This is an ideal salad to serve with grilled meat or fish, or as a distinctly Korean potluck dish.

DRESSING

¼ cup minced white onion

1 Korean red chile, half minced and half thinly sliced and kept separate

1 tablespoon rice vinegar

1 teaspoon soy sauce

1 teaspoon fish sauce

1 teaspoon honey

½ teaspoon peeled, grated fresh ginger

½ teaspoon gochugaru

½ teaspoon kosher salt

1 tablespoon extra-virgin olive oil

1 teaspoon sesame oil

4 tangerines

2 tablespoons toasted pine nuts, roughly chopped

Spicy microgreens, for garnish

1 **Make the dressing:** In a small bowl, stir together the onion, minced chile, vinegar, soy sauce, fish sauce, honey, ginger, gochugaru, and salt until the salt dissolves. Add both oils and stir to mix well.

2 Peel the tangerines, pulling off any excess pith, and slice into rounds. Remove and discard any seeds.

3 Arrange the tangerine rounds in a single layer on a serving platter. Spoon the dressing evenly on top. Sprinkle with the pine nuts and chile slices, garnish with microgreens, and serve.

Who Are the Haenyeo? A Deeper Dive

One of the biggest surprises to us over the past decade has been the increased visibility of the haenyeo, Jeju's female seafood and seaweed divers, in pop culture, including both scripted and documentary films, long articles in publications like *The New Yorker*, and even an off-Broadway play presented in 2020.

But how did it begin? The history of this community of free divers, some working late into their sixties, has been passed through many sources, and it can be difficult to distinguish between fact and lore. One theory suggests that the female population turned to diving because so many men had been lost at sea. Another attributes the phenomenon to women anatomically having a higher shivering threshold than men, making them better equipped for cold-water diving.

We asked Nadia Cho, a longtime friend of ours, who is working on a documentary film on the aging divers. She says the haenyeo are more a symbol of survival. "Jeju is surrounded by natural enemies and has been invaded for centuries. With wars, the men would often head off to battle and not return," she explains. With fishing as the primary, if not the sole, industry on the island, mothers and daughters were asked to pick up the slack.

Traditional haenyeo free diving forces the divers to risk their lives nearly every day. A routine dive to collect abalone, octopus, and various species of seaweed has the diver plunging to a depth of nearly one hundred feet. On a visit to the Jeju Haenyeo Museum on the island's far eastern coast, we walk past glass cases holding the extremely bare-bones gear (thin cotton swimming dresses and ill-fitting goggles) that the haenyeo have used over the past seventy-five years.

Cho is drawn to documenting the haenyeo because she sees the need to tell a deeper story that goes beyond the feats of endurance. Some could say the rise in the haenyeo visibility in popular culture dovetails with a rise in female empowerment for Koreans worldwide, pushing back against the traditional patriarchal culture. And what better symbol than a tough-as-nails diver—self-assured and self-sufficient. There's also the simple fact that haenyeo diving is truly an act of mind over matter, and offers a tidy tale of enduring adversity. "There's a lot of philosophy to learn from their lives, and that goes beyond just holding your breath," Cho says.

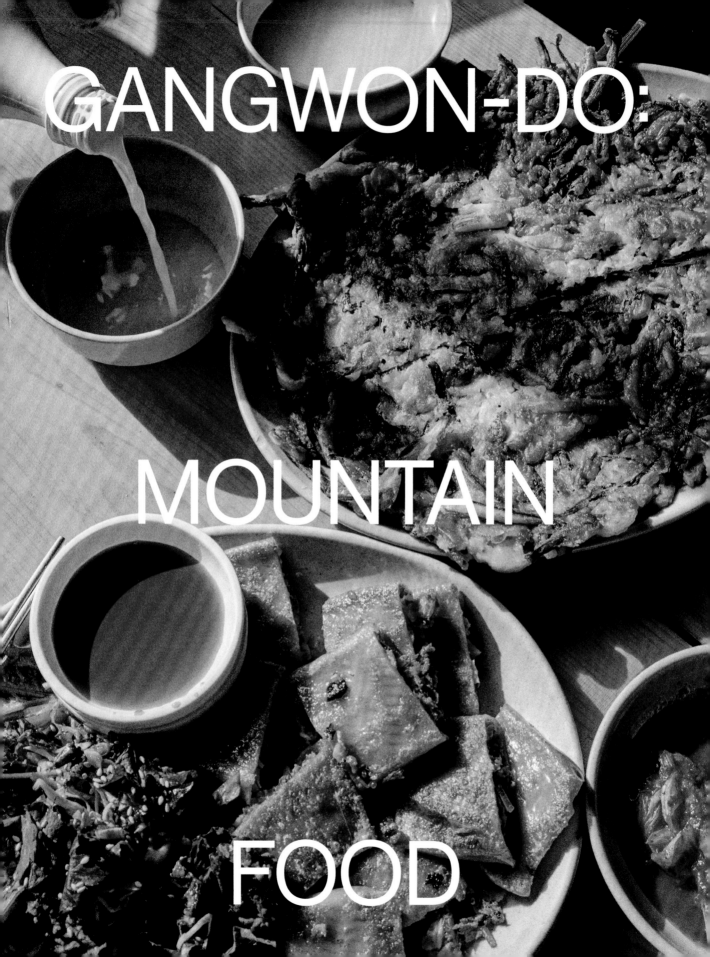

GANGWON-DO:
MOUNTAIN
FOOD

Located in the northeastern corner of the Korean peninsula, Gangwon-do is a remote and mountainous region famous for its natural parks, pristine beaches, and winter sports and activities. The 2018 Winter Olympics took place in Pyeongchang, and thanks to the rural region's place on the world stage through those events, improved roads and high-speed trains have made it very accessible to anybody visiting Seoul, with the trip now taking under two hours. This slim chapter gives you a taste of a region that is ripe for exploration.

Hiking is a near-national pastime in Korea, and on a visit to Seoraksan National Park on a sparkling December day in 2022, we saw this passion play out in living color. After boarding a luxury coach in Seoul (for under $20 to boot), we found ourselves just two hours later at a rental car counter in the seaside town of Sokcho. Following a short drive, we were within the park gates, battling the lines of Genesis sedans and eventually walking along clearly marked paths, over bridges, and past the Great Unification Buddha, the largest seated bronze Buddha statue in the world at nearly five stories high. Dotting the paths were several cafés serving makgeolli (a milky, slightly sparkling rice wine) and jeon (pancakes), which have traditionally been paired with hiking activities throughout Korea.

And while we were there for the food and the sunny skies, it was the parade of Arc'teryx, Snow Peak, and North Face that had us most impressed. Hiking 'fits in Korea are on another level, and the dedication to dressing in the most modern performance gear seems like the main objective.

In this chapter, we offer two dishes that we learned about while doing our own alpine explorations inside Seoraksan National Park: bibim guksu, made with Gangwon-do's iconic buckwheat noodles, and memil jeonbyeong, a buckwheat pancake roll filled with sautéed spicy napa cabbage kimchi. Yum.

BIBIM GUKSU
CHILLED BUCKWHEAT NOODLES WITH VINEGAR AND LEMON-LIME SODA SAUCE
비빔국수

SERVES 4

This spicy and chilled noodle salad is built around chewy buckwheat noodles and a refreshing sauce that brings together gochujang, vinegar, and the iconic industrial sweetness of American lemon-lime soda (either Sprite or 7UP will do, and you can even sub in ginger ale). Buckwheat noodles or, as they are known most commonly in their Japanese form, soba, are in Korea widely associated with the Gangwon region, where the local buckwheat harvest is turned into springy, nutty noodles that have more intensity than most commercially available soba. Bibim guksu is a perfect, refreshing lunch for a sticky summer afternoon. During a swampy and sweltering heat wave, you can even top each bowl of noodles with crushed ice. And if you cannot find Gangwon-do buckwheat noodles, high-quality soba or even somen (wheat noodles) will work.

SAUCE

¼ cup gochujang

2 tablespoons coarsely ground gochugaru

¼ cup soy sauce

¼ cup grated Asian pear or apple

¼ cup sugar or Fruit Preserves (see page 149)

⅓ cup Sprite or 7UP

⅓ cup cider vinegar or rice vinegar

6 garlic cloves, grated

1 pound thin buckwheat noodles

¼ cup thinly sliced red cabbage

¼ cup thinly sliced cucumber

¼ cup peeled, thinly sliced carrot

¼ cup grated Korean radish or daikon

1 Asian pear, halved and thinly sliced

1 tablespoon sesame seeds, plus more for garnish

2 perilla or shiso leaves, thinly sliced

4 eggs, soft-boiled and halved lengthwise

¼ cup crushed ice (optional)

1 **Make the sauce:** In a small bowl, whisk together all the ingredients until well mixed and free of clumps.

2 Have ready a large bowl of ice water. Bring a large pot of water to a boil over high heat. Add the noodles and cook according to the package instructions. Drain well, then shock them in the ice water. Once the noodles are well chilled, drain thoroughly.

3 Transfer the cold noodles to a large bowl or platter. Arrange the cabbage, cucumber, carrot, radish, and ¾ cup of the pear over the noodles. Top with the sauce.

4 Garnish with the sesame seeds, perilla, eggs, and remaining pear. Bring the dish to the table for the grand reveal, then toss everything together. If you like, top with the ice for the ultimate chilled noodles.

FRUIT PRESERVES / NATURAL FRUIT SWEETENER
과일청

MAKES 2 CUPS

When we were writing *Koreatown*, we often leaned into rice syrup when we needed to add a hint of sweetness. Times have changed, and over the past decade, many home cooks and Korean chefs, Deuki included, have started keeping cheong on hand, particularly maesil (Korean green plum) cheong, which we have incorporated into a number of recipes. In Korean cooking, cheong is a sweet fruit preserve that's between a syrup and a jam, and it's often used diluted as a hot or cold tea or to flavor everything from bulgogi and fish jorims (braises) to salad dressing and kimchi. Here are a number of ways to make cheong using the golden ratio as the base.

GOLDEN RATIO

1 cup fruit of choice (see below)

¾ cup pure cane sugar

1 tablespoon fresh lemon or lime juice

1 tablespoon kosher salt

FRUIT OPTIONS

Strawberries: Hulled, then halved.

Maesil (Green Plum): Halved, pitted, and diced; no need to peel.

Orange: Peeled and diced.

Kiwi: Peeled and diced.

Lemon: Peeled and diced.

1   In a medium bowl, combine all the ingredients and stir well. Cover and keep at room temperature for about 24 hours, stirring once or twice. The mixture is ready when all the sugar has dissolved in the fruit's natural juices.

2   Transfer the fruit and its juices to a sterilized jar, cap tightly, and place in the refrigerator to age for 3 days to 1 month. It's important to stir every day or so, especially during the first week, to prevent a hard sugar crust from forming on the top. The harder the fruit, such as green plums, the longer it will take to age. Check it daily as it ages. At the end of the process, the fruit will have broken down (feel free to strain out any remaining peels) and you will be left with a sweet-tart syrup that is perfect for all styles of cooking. Cheong can be stored unrefrigerated in an airtight container for a year or more.

MEMIL JEONBYEONG
SPICY KIMCHI BUCKWHEAT PANCAKE ROLL
메밀전병

SERVES 2 OR 3

Up in Gangwon-do, along with winter sports and exceptional seafood, buckwheat flourishes and has been literally baked into the cuisine for generations. One of the specialty foods is this lesser-known, amazing pancake roll. It looks deceptively like it could be a mild affair – mostly spongy buckwheat carrying the dish. But the filling is typically a very spicy baechu (napa cabbage) kimchi that is heated up with plenty of gochugaru. After we went hiking in Seoraksan National Park, we stopped by a small restaurant just off the path. There, we had a memil jeonbyeong that blew our minds: a springy buckwheat pancake wrapped tightly around sautéed napa cabbage kimchi and then lightly panfried. We knew we had to include the recipe here.

1 **Make the pancake batter:** In a medium bowl, whisk together both flours and the salt. Add the water and sesame oil and whisk gently until there are no lumps. The batter should have the consistency of a very thin pancake batter. Add more water if it's too thick. Let rest at room temperature for at least 30 minutes or up to an hour.

2 **Make the filling:** While the batter rests, bring a small saucepan filled with water to a boil over high heat, add the noodles, and boil until tender, 6 to 7 minutes. Drain and rinse under cold running water, then shake well and squeeze out as much water as possible. Chop into short segments with a knife or snip with kitchen scissors. Transfer to a large bowl. Add the tofu, soy sauce, and the ½ teaspoon of the sesame oil to the noodles and mix well.

3 In a large skillet, heat the remaining 1 tablespoon sesame oil over medium-high heat until it shimmers. Add the kimchi and cook, stirring occasionally, until it is dry and starting to brown at the edges, 4 to 5 minutes. Add the garlic and cook, stirring, until translucent, about 2 minutes. Stir in the scallions, gochugaru, sesame seeds, and sugar, mixing well, and remove from the heat. Transfer to the bowl with the noodles and tofu. Stir until well combined and season with salt and pepper. Rinse and dry the skillet.

4 **Make the dipping sauce:** In a small bowl, combine the soy sauce and vinegar and mix well.

5 **Cook and fill the pancakes:** Place the skillet over medium-high heat and add 1 to 2 teaspoons neutral oil. When the oil shimmers, pour about ⅓ cup of the batter into the center of the pan and, using the back of a spoon, immediately start spreading it out into a thin circle (about 7 inches in diameter). Cook until lightly browned on the underside, 30 seconds to 1 minute, then flip the pancake.

PANCAKE
¾ cup light (hulled) buckwheat flour

¼ cup all-purpose flour

½ teaspoon kosher salt

1¼ cups water, plus more as needed

1 teaspoon sesame oil

Neutral cooking oil, for cooking

FILLING
1 ounce sweet potato (glass) noodles (about ½ cup when cooked)

4 ounces medium or firm tofu, squeezed dry

1 teaspoon soy sauce

1 tablespoon plus ½ teaspoon sesame oil

1½ cups drained napa cabbage kimchi, sliced into thin strips

3 garlic cloves, minced

2 scallions, white and green parts, sliced

1 tablespoon gochugaru

1 tablespoon toasted sesame seeds

½ teaspoon sugar

Kosher salt and ground black pepper

DIPPING SAUCE
2 tablespoons soy sauce

2 tablespoons rice vinegar

6   Arrange a heaping ¼ cup of the filling in a log shape on the bottom third of the pancake in the skillet, leaving about 1 inch uncovered on either side. Using two spatulas, and starting from the edge, roll the pancake tightly around the filling, leaving the sides open. Gently press down on the sides to seal. Cook the rolled pancake, turning once, until browned and crisp on both sides, 1 to 2 minutes per side. Transfer to a platter and cover loosely with foil to keep warm. Repeat with the remaining batter and filling.

7   Cut each rolled pancake into four pieces and arrange on a platter. Serve with the dipping sauce.

02

THE NEW KOREATOWN

While our travels in contemporary Korea have been filled with stories and recipes rooted in the deep past as well as the evolving present, for us, the story of Koreatowns in the United States is all about what's new right now. A decade after we began reporting on the country's Koreatowns—mostly in the hubs of Atlanta, Los Angeles, and New York—there's been incredible growth and changes in trends and tastes that make the subject rich for new exploration.

The story of the boom of Korean restaurants of all styles throughout the United States has been one of the biggest, if not *the biggest*, story in food over the past several years.

Chefs of all backgrounds have embraced contemporary Korean cooking ideas—some of which we cover in the book's first section—and packaged them sharply for astute US diners. And while this tale has played out in the pages of Eater, *Bon Appétit*, and the *New York Times*, for every innovative chef like Eunjo Park or Roy Choi, there are many more lesser-known Korean American chefs, farmers, bakers, bartenders, and small business owners writing a new story. This section is a tribute to the spirit of Korean food in the United States during the past decade, a time of great opportunity for, and opportunity embraced by, Korean Americans everywhere.

WHAT IT
MEANS

TO COOK
KOREAN

TODAY

To answer this question concisely is a fool's errand, and thankfully we have the space to give it our best shot through a selection of recipes that offers many different points of view. As we noted in the book's introduction, we are not writing an encyclopedia of the Korean canon of soups, stews, and grilled meats. We did that already in our last book, *Koreatown*. Instead, the reporting of this book took us from coast to coast in search of creativity and, ultimately, deliciousness that stretches the definition of Korean food.

In this chapter, we catch up with some of the freshest voices in Korean food, including Ted and Yong Kim of Seoul Sausage Company. They tell us about their booming boxed-lunch business and how a no-compromise approach to Korean-style cooking (and naming convention) has earned the company a strong reputation in the city with the country's largest Korean diasporic population. (Netflix, the most popular platform of Korean dramas, is a client.)

We meet former education and tech executives Eddo Kim and Clara Lee, who run the online grocery Queens SF and find out how they have been changing the perception of the Korean grocery store—think small-scale imports from Korea that serve as a direct link to the artisanship happening three thousand miles away.

Former Momofuku chef Eunjo Park gives us a serious kimbap lesson while showing that the Korean rice roll is the perfect vehicle for creativity. We speak with journalist Matthew Kang about his native Los Angeles, a city that is seeing a crashing together of old and new, and we seek out chef and stylist Susan Kim to talk pickles—outrageously delicious pickles. We've been inspired by so many stories and recipes, and this chapter is filled with both. This is a journey, and we hope you're excited to ride along with us.

What does it all add up to? To us, Korean food in America today is the holding of a deeply rooted point of view (that is, cooking honestly for one's self) while always thinking about the big picture—keeping the fickle restaurant-goer interested and coming back for more. We encountered dishes that challenged us and others that were mined from cultures outside of Korea (see our sidebar explaining the idea of fusion cuisine). And we met a cast of characters that will be answering this question for years to come.

30-MINUTE JOKBAL
30 분 족발

SERVES 4

These deeply flavorful, marinated pigs' trotters are usually seen as one of the icons in the canon of anju (drinking foods). But seeing jokbal as merely a snack to pair with soju sells the dish way short. It's one of the best Korean foods, period.

We avoided writing a recipe for it in our first book because, frankly, the process of cooking down the pigs' feet to the ideal jellylike consistency is a real art that we weren't ready to tackle. And unless you live near a large Asian market, finding the perfect pigs' feet could prove challenging.

This leads to our final point: we wanted to write a recipe that channeled all the reasons we love jokbal – the inky soy sauce marinade, the warming spices, the perfect texture of the skin – but without the trotters and the hours of braising. So we thought, "What if Rachael Ray made a thirty-minute Braised Pork in the Style of Jokbal?" (Just to be clear, this is not a Rachael Ray recipe, but we miss the show, RR!) Our pared-down process uses skin-on pork butt, which gets at the richness of jokbal but has a chewier texture. We call for a few key ingredients, including the thicker and slightly sweeter dark Chinese soy sauce and tingly Sichuan peppercorns. Once you've secured them, the iconic jokbal flavor will be yours.

1 tablespoon neutral cooking oil

2 pounds skin-on boneless pork butt or picnic ham, cut into 1-inch pieces

Sea salt

10 garlic cloves

3-inch knob fresh ginger, peeled and sliced

3 to 4 scallions, white and green parts, thinly sliced

Ssamjang (page 91), for serving

SAUCE

4 cups water

½ cup sake or soju

½ cup soy sauce

2 tablespoons Chinese dark soy sauce (lǎo chōu)

2 tablespoons dark brown sugar

1 cinnamon stick

2 whole star anise pods

6 Sichuan peppercorns

1 In a large sauté pan or Dutch oven, heat the oil over medium-high heat until it shimmers. Season the pork pieces with salt and place skin side down in the pan to start. Sizzle the pork pieces, turning them every few minutes, until golden brown all over, about 10 minutes. Add the garlic and ginger and cook, stirring, until fragrant, about 3 minutes.

2 **Make the sauce:** While the pork cooks, in a medium bowl, whisk together all the ingredients until well mixed.

3 When the pork is ready, pour the sauce over the pork and adjust the heat to maintain a strong simmer. Let simmer until the sauce is reduced by more than half to a saucy, syrupy consistency and the pork is tender, about 15 minutes.

4 Transfer the pork and sauce to a serving dish, top with the scallions, and serve immediately, with the ssamjang on the side.

"OH, YUK FANCY, HUH?" YUKHWE
육회

SERVES 4

How do we take the perfect combination of raw beef, seasoned soy sauce, orchard fruit, and eggs to a higher level? How can Deuki use his fine-dining chops, honed at Jean-Georges back in the day, to rethink this classic dish? Of course, traditional yukhwe doesn't need to be "elevated," but let this version serve as a symbol for how Korea's fine-dining game has expanded dramatically over the past decade. Deuki's answer is the salt-cured egg, which adds a salty richness to the marinated beef. Note that this step takes a few days of planning — that is, the egg needs to cure in the refrigerator. The result is both delicious and visually stunning. In fact, your dinner guests may just utter, "Oh, yuk fancy, huh?"

DRESSING

3 tablespoons soy sauce

1 tablespoon sesame oil

1 tablespoon gochujang

1 tablespoon honey

1 pound beef tenderloin, chilled and diced small

½ Asian pear, peeled and diced small

1 teaspoon toasted sesame seeds

4 Salt-Cured Egg Yolks (recipe follows; made 4 to 5 days in advance)

2 tablespoons finely chopped fresh chives, for garnish

1   **Make the dressing:** In a medium bowl, combine all the ingredients and stir until smooth.

2   Add the beef, pear, and sesame seeds to the dressing and toss to mix well. Allow to marinate for 10 minutes.

3   Divide the beef mixture among four chilled plates, arranging it neatly in the center of each plate.

4   Grate an egg yolk over each beef portion. Garnish with chives and serve immediately.

Salt-Cured Egg Yolks
소금 절임 노른자

These salt-cured yolks add a yolky richness and savoriness to a number of dishes beyond yukhwe, including pastas, salads, and soups.

2 cups kosher salt

2 tablespoons sugar

2 tablespoons coarsely ground gochugaru

1 tablespoon garlic powder

4 eggs

1   In a small bowl, mix together the salt, sugar, gochugaru, and garlic powder. Spread half of the salt mixture in a shallow pan.

2   Separate an egg and carefully lay the yolk on top of the salt mixture. Reserve the white for another use. Repeat with the remaining eggs, spacing the yolks 3 to 4 inches apart. Carefully cover the yolks with the remaining salt mixture, making sure not to break them. Cover the pan and refrigerate for 4 to 5 days. The cured egg yolks are ready when they are firm and easy to handle.

3   Take the yolks out of the salt mixture and rinse with cold water. Preheat the oven to the lowest temperature it can hold (ideally 180°F). Line a sheet pan with parchment paper or a silicone mat and place the yolks on the prepared pan. Warm the yolks for 2 hours.

4   Remove the yolks from the oven and let cool. They are now ready to use.

DANNY AND YESOON LEE ARE THE MAYORS OF NORTHERN VIRGINIA AND WASHINGTON, DC, KOREATOWNS

"It was our family dream to open a Korean restaurant in the District," Danny Lee says between bites of jorim, slow-braised red snapper and Korean radish, that he and his mother (and business partner),Yesoon, had prepared on a hot summer afternoon. "There wasn't a strictly Korean restaurant in Washington, DC, which was absolutely crazy." The year was 2006, and Danny and Yesoon had been building toward the moment they would open Mandu, the first act in what is now a legitimate empire of restaurants in the Washington–Maryland–Northern Virginia region.

Northern Virginia has, like New York City up the road, long been a hub for Korean immigration, establishing vibrant communities around Centreville and Annandale. The Korean community in Virginia and in nearby Washington, DC, and Maryland is the third largest in the United States, spiking sharply in the 1990s due to a variety of factors, including the increase in nonstop flights to and from Korea, the general affordability of the region (compared with New York and Los Angeles), and the proximity to government jobs and the Korean Embassy.

Yesoon had been a member of the community since moving to the area with her husband, Jong Koo Lee, in 1976. When Jong Koo unexpectedly passed while Danny was a freshman in high school, the newly widowed homemaker was forced to find a job to support her two children. Food service was a natural fit for the skilled home cook, and Yesoon eventually teamed up with DC restaurateur Charlie Chiang to open a Chinese fast-casual restaurant, Charlie Chiang's Kwai, in the new Reagan National airport in the late '90s. The business thrived for nearly a decade, until the young Danny, who graduated from the University of Virginia and then spent time at the Department of Defense, a law firm, and eventually restaurant management, proposed the Mandu idea, named in tribute to his mother's dumplings.

Opening in a former Nepalese restaurant in Dupont Circle, the Lees soon established the restaurant—and themselves—as the founding figures of Washington, DC, Koreatown. It wasn't easy. "We fell on our faces the first

six months," Danny admits, citing the difficulty in scaling up Yesoon's family dishes, like pork mandu, dak jjim, and bibimbap, that had been staples in their Northern Virginia home. "I also underestimated the size of the magnifying glass we would be viewed through. I was young and cocky, and I thought I knew everything, which I didn't." And the dynamic of mother and son running a restaurant was straining at times. Danny tells the story of a curse word being uttered and his mom throwing her apron toward him and threatening to walk home to Vienna, Virginia. "There was a generational gap that we had to overcome," Yesoon admits. Danny cuts in, "Her generation thought that a Korean restaurant should be open for breakfast, lunch, and dinner every day, no matter what the cost was. This wasn't going to work."

The two eventually talked it out, and as the years passed—and Korean food's profile rose within the less-than-adventurous DC food circles—Mandu thrived, and Danny expanded to open the award-winning Anju with Angel Barreto (see page 226) and a chain of fast-casual Chinese and Korean restaurants (Chiko) with the chef Scott Drewno. James Beard Foundation awards followed, and Danny is hardly slowing down—with broad expansion plans riding the Korean Wave. "We want to open two a year," Danny says of future plans for Chiko. But the energy and drive are still centered at Mandu, and Yesoon, now seventy-six, is ever present in the kitchen, tasting sauces and teaching new staff to prepare the namesake dumplings. "I never knew how restaurant food should taste," Yesoon says with a smile. "I knew the taste my family enjoyed."

Obviously, the family has pretty great taste, and DC is lucky to have such accomplished restaurants flying the Korean flag. "We learned to trust our own palates and memories, as opposed to listening to other people's feedback." Danny says. "And no one knows better than her," he adds, pointing at his mother before returning to the fish jorim the elder Lee had prepared for us all to enjoy.

SAENGSEON MU JORIM
BRAISED FISH AND RADISH
생선무우조림

SERVES 2 OR 3

This recipe arrives from the kitchen of the mother-son duo of Yesoon and Danny Lee, chef-owners of Mandu, Washington, DC's pioneering modern Korean restaurant. We've long been fans of their restaurants, and Danny kindly hosted us for a raucous after-party following a *Koreatown* book event ten years ago. While Yesoon's mandus are naturally legendary, one dish that stuck in our heads was jorim, fish and radish slowly braised in a powerfully pungent sauce of gochujang and doenjang, fish and soy sauces, mirin, and soju. The cooked fish, light and absorbing the sauce, plays well with the fork-tender radish, which is still slightly sweet and vegetal. This is pure Korean home cooking.

While this works well with any white fish like snapper or branzino, the radish can also be served solo. Slow-cooked radish is a long-standing Korean tradition, and preparing it in this sauce is the perfect example of why.

SAUCE

¾ cup soy sauce

3 tablespoons mirin

3 tablespoons soju

2 tablespoons fish sauce

6 tablespoons coarsely ground gochugaru

2 tablespoons gochujang

1 tablespoon doenjang

3-inch knob fresh ginger, peeled and minced

6 garlic cloves, minced

3 tablespoons sugar

1 pound Korean radish or daikon, peeled, cut into 1-inch-thick wheels, and wheels halved

4 cups Anchovy Stock (page 47), vegetable stock, or water

½ white onion, thinly sliced

Two 8-ounce fillets skin-on branzino, red snapper, or other white fish

1 Korean green chile, thinly sliced

1 bunch scallions, white and green parts, sliced

Hot cooked short-grain rice, for serving

1   **Make the sauce:** In a small bowl, stir together all the ingredients until well mixed and the sugar dissolves.

2   Place the radish pieces in a single layer in a large, sauté pan or shallow saucepan and pour in enough stock to cover the pieces.

3   Add about one-third of the sauce and mix with the stock and radish pieces. Bring to a boil, cover, and then turn down the heat to medium-low. Baste and turn the radish pieces occasionally as it reduces and drops below the tops of the pieces, about 20 minutes.

4   At this point, the braising liquid should have reduced by about half. Add more stock to bring to a level even with the top of the radish pieces. Add the onion, distributing the slices evenly across the radish pieces and stock.

5   Cut the fish fillets in half on the diagonal and place, skin side up, on top of the radish pieces and onion. They should sit mostly above the liquid. Using a spoon, cover the fish pieces with about half of the remaining sauce.

6   Raise the heat to high and bring the liquid to a boil, then immediately lower the heat to a simmer, cover, and braise the fish, basting it with the braising liquid every 2 minutes or so. After about 7 minutes, spoon the remaining sauce on top of the fish and add the chile and half of the scallions, distributing them evenly across the top of the pan.

7   Re-cover and simmer until the fish is cooked, about 2 minutes longer. Then remove from the heat, garnish with the remaining scallions, and serve immediately with rice.

A LOS ANGELES HANG WITH KOREATOWN RUN CLUB

Neither Duy Nguyen nor Mike Pak was a runner when they started LA's Koreatown Run Club in 2016, growing a community that now hosts organized runs around the neighborhood (and beyond) several days a week. Pak is one of the loudest young voices of Koreatown and the spirit behind the creative and Zeitgeist-tapping @koreatown Instagram account. Nguyen, who works in film, got interested in organizing a group after returning from a documentary shoot in Haiti, where he observed ultramarathoners running two hundred miles over the course of a week. "They were like regular people and not professional athletes," Nguyen recalls while sipping an iced latte at Document Coffee Bar, a Korean-owned café off Wilshire Boulevard. "They were like, 'We're going to do this,' and they raised a bunch of money in the process." After hearing the story from his old college friend, Pak put a simple message out on his heavily followed IG account: "Meet at the LINE Hotel on Saturday. The run club is on."

Twenty people showed up for that first run, and many more for the next. For Koreatown, this has meant a few things: a way to link the love of running with the neighborhood; a reason to drink beers after a good sweat. But mainly the club is an easy way to bring together Korean Americans, and friends of Korean Americans, living in one of the country's most vital Korean communities.

We asked Nguyen why he likes to run, and he admitted that it's everything but the actual running. But for the record, he had run a slick seven marathons the previous year and is personally organizing most of the weekly runs around Wilshire, out west sometimes all the way to Santa Monica, and meeting at the track at Los Angeles City College every so often. "It's not about the miles but about connecting with the people we get to meet each week," he explained. Nguyen and Pak also run the burger and fries pop-up Love Hour, housed in the former (and legendary) Koreatown beer garden Beer Belly, and Thursday runs end with a happy hour.

We've been fans of @koreatown for a long time, and we wanted to find out how running the Instagram account has brought the community together—and where they are eating. "In the early years, the one restaurant we went to was Escala," says Pak of the Chapman Plaza restaurant and bar that mashes Colombian and Korean flavors. "Oh, yeah, and Dan Sung Sa," Nguyen jumps in with a little smile, referring to an iconic pojangmacha, or late-night bar, that serves a robust menu of hearty bar food. Everybody who has ever been to the Sixth Street pocha (late-night bar) has a story or three. And the future? "We're not doing an NFT thing," Nguyen jokes. "And we aren't doing an internet thing," Pak says. "We are just trying to be a part of it and in the mix."

KOREAN CHICKEN TERIYAKI
한국식 치킨 데리야끼

SERVES 4

Teriyaki is firmly rooted in Japanese cooking tradition, dating back to the seventeenth century and arriving in the United States first via Hawaii at the end of the nineteenth century. But as photo editor and journalist Will Matsuda reported in a memorable story for *TASTE*, "teriyaki remains Japanese in name only," particularly in the Pacific Northwest, where Korean Americans run the most popular teriyaki stands in Seattle and Portland. At these establishments, the deeply marinated meat (mostly chicken) lands somewhere between bulgogi and the more traditional bento-box staple found in other parts of the country.

Matsuda introduced us to Anthony Park, who has been running Portland's legendary Du's Grill since 2009, when he took it over from his parents, Bae and Muncha Park. Park compares a takeout box of grilled chicken in Portland to pizza in New York and tacos in Los Angeles, and on any given afternoon, the lines slink out of his two locations, in Northeast Portland and in the Portland suburb of Hillsboro. While Park has not shared his exact family recipe, he was cool enough to give us a really great version that is pretty damn close.

MARINADE

1 cup soy sauce

1 cup sugar

¼ teaspoon ground ginger

½ teaspoon garlic powder

¼ teaspoon ground black pepper

3 tablespoons pineapple juice

2 tablespoons mirin

Kosher salt

1½ pounds boneless, skinless chicken thighs

2 tablespoons neutral cooking oil

Kosher salt and ground white pepper

Sesame seeds, for garnish

Cooked short-grain rice, for serving

1. **Make the marinade:** In a small saucepan, combine the soy sauce, sugar, ginger, garlic powder, black pepper, pineapple juice, and mirin and whisk to mix well and dissolve the sugar. Season with salt, place over high heat, and bring to a boil, stirring often. Drop the heat to a simmer and simmer until the marinade just begins to thicken, 3 to 4 minutes. Remove from the heat and let cool to room temperature.

2. In a medium bowl, toss the chicken with half of the marinade, coating well. Tightly cover the bowl, or transfer the chicken and its marinade to a large ziplock bag and seal closed. Marinate the chicken in the refrigerator for at least 2 hours or up to 2 days.

3. Remove the chicken from the marinade, discarding the marinade. Cut the chicken against the grain into bite-size strips. In a large skillet, heat the oil over medium-high heat until it shimmers. Add the chicken in a single layer and season with salt and white pepper. Cook until the chicken is nearly done and golden brown on the underside, 2 to 3 minutes. Flip and continue to cook until cooked through, 1 to 2 minutes. Season again with salt and white pepper and transfer to a plate.

4. Pour the remaining marinade into the skillet, place over medium-high heat, bring to a boil, and deglaze the pan, stirring to dislodge all the browned bits (the fond) from the pan bottom. Return the chicken to the skillet, toss to coat thoroughly, and remove from the heat.

5. Transfer the chicken to a serving dish, garnish with sesame seeds, and serve immediately with rice.

SUSAN KIM
DREAMS OF DOSHI

"All of these warm, positive, tender memories are about food." Susan Kim, a roving pop-up chef and go-to recipe developer, was born in Gangnam, the ultra-luxurious neighborhood in the southern part of Seoul that her mom jokes was "just dirt back then." But Kim's time living in Korea was a brief seven years, and her memories are limited to visiting the local spot for samgyeopsal (grilled pork belly) and grocery shopping. "For Korean kids, the way we grew up eating made us instinctual cooks because we grew up flipping meat. We're looking for the right color and flipping until it is exactly ready."

Knowing how to avoid the crusty, burnt edges of overfired bulgogi has served Kim well in her choice of career. She grew up first in Queens, New York, and later outside of Los Angeles, eating the food of her mom's home of Jeolla-do ("so in your face and powerfully delicious"), and the fragrant jeotgal and raw oysters that would heavily season the family's baechu (napa cabbage) kimchi made a big impression. Her grandfather was a cook in the US Army, so milk and butter were often used in their house, a rare occurrence for a Korean family at that time, and something that shaped Susan's mom into the "audacious" cook that would come to fuse Mexican and Korean flavors well before the world was hip to the ways of Roy Choi and Kogi BBQ. "Everything could be banchan," she says, noting that slices of American cheese and cocktail olives would find their way onto the family table as a predinner blast of salt to wake up the appetite. "It's no different from jangjorim," she says of the traditional banchan of boiled beef and soy sauce.

Kim's professional cooking career has taken her around the world. She was at Berkeley's famed Chez Panisse for many years and helped open the Michelin-starred Agern and the modern Korean pocha, Insa, in New York City, as well as working as a food stylist. But it wasn't until she founded the pop-up Doshi (short for *dosirak*, or Korean lunchbox, and *dosi*, meaning "city") in 2019 that she really started to explore Korean boxed meals as their own exciting category, merging her interests in Korean food, design, and community. "It's such a sensory experience and similar to opening up a gift," she says of the diner's unboxing moment. After the events of 2020 hit ("a time of quiet both workwise and in my head"), it was near the year's end that Kim realized it was game on, and Doshi was born into the world.

Attending Doshi is a vibe, and Kim has partnered with some of the most exciting names in food, including Superiority Burger and MeMe's Diner in New York (RIP), Kismet in Los Angeles, Queens in San Francisco, and Early June in Paris. Boxes and à la carte dinners show the Susan Kim way of flexing the versatility of doenjang (she uses it to braise eggplant) and serving traditional raw fish (hwe) scooped with crispy fish-skin chips. She has made a version of soondae (more like a British-styled blood cake) with dangmyun (sweet potato noodles), perilla, and chanterelle mushroom gravy, and a modern tteokbokki with grilled halloumi. If and when the time comes for Kim to open a restaurant, it will unarguably be an exciting event—and a real moment for Korean food. Susan Kim is a strong voice in modern Korean cooking, and her exciting future plans cannot be put into a single box—unless, of course, it's in dosirak form.

SESAME OIL PICKLES
참기름채소장아찌

MAKES 3 QUARTS

Giardiniera is the Italian term for pickled vegetables in zippy vinegar, with a few pours of olive oil thrown in for good measure. For fans of the ur-restaurant television drama *The Bear*, you will know the importance of giardiniera in building a Chicago Italian beef sandwich. And for fans of Chicago foods writ large, you will know the importance of giardiniera in topping the city's preferred pizza style, tavern, at places like Pat's Pizza and Milly's Pizza in the Pan. If you know pizza, you know the Windy City is a tavern town and the only order is giardiniera and sausage.

So what does this have to do with Korean food? Susan Kim is a chef and recipe developer who has worked in fine dining and more soulful places like Berkeley's Chez Panisse and Brooklyn's Insa (see page 172). Her world-traveling Doshi pop-ups are very popular, and when we got to talking about recipes that inspire her, a Korean version of giardiniera hit the top of the list. Bracingly sweet and licoricey fennel, candy-sweet carrots, and pleasantly vegetal radish bridge Korea and America in a really cool way, and once pickled in a sweetened vinegar and a good amount of sesame oil, they make for a crunchy banchan to serve with a jjigae or grilled fish. When we hung out at Susan's Brooklyn apartment, she made this with cherry tomatoes, sugar snap peas, and baby turnips, so feel free to experiment by swapping in your favorite vegetables.

3 medium carrots (about 1 pound)

3 medium fennel bulbs

1 pound Korean radish or daikon

4 cups water

3 cups rice vinegar

½ cup sugar

2 tablespoons kosher salt

½ cup sesame oil

2 tablespoons gochugaru

2 tablespoons fennel seeds

2 tablespoons sesame seeds, plus more for garnish

1 Peel the carrots, then julienne into 2-inch-long pieces. Cut the fronds off the fennel bulbs, chop roughly, and reserve. Remove the tough outer layers from the bulbs, then halve lengthwise, place the halves cut side down, and cut crosswise into ¼-inch-thick pieces. Peel the daikon, halve it lengthwise, place the halves cut side down, and slice them as thinly as possible into half-moons. Stack the half-moons and cut in half to form quarter rounds.

2 In a medium saucepan, bring the water, vinegar, sugar, and salt to a boil over medium heat.

3 Meanwhile, in a large, heatproof bowl, whisk together the oil, gochugaru, fennel seeds, sesame seeds, and reserved fennel fronds.

4 Once the pickling liquid comes to a boil, add the carrots, fennel, and daikon and blanch for 1½ minutes, then drain well. If the pot isn't big enough to hold all the vegetables at once, blanch each type separately, scooping out each one with a slotted spoon or spider as it is ready. Add the blanched vegetables to the bowl with the oil mixture and toss to coat evenly. Pour the hot pickling liquid over the vegetables and toss again.

5 Transfer the vegetables and their liquid to one or two large jars, three quart-size jars, or several small jars. Let cool uncovered at room temperature for 1 hour. Seal with a lid and refrigerate. The pickles will be ready to eat the next day. They will keep refrigerated for up to 2 months.

6 Before serving, give the pickles a quick toss, as the oil may have pooled on top. Serve with more sesame seeds sprinkled on top.

GRILLED KIMCHI WEDGE SALAD
구운김치샐러드

SERVES 4

This playful side dish is inspired by two of Deuki's great loves: braised tofu with kimchi and the American steak-house classic, the wedge salad. It's perfect paired with a grilled rib eye for a summer cookout. Kimchi lovers know that kimchi takes on a new form when grilled, transforming from sharply flavored to gently sour like a dill pickle. The creamy, velvety tofu-based dressing, which is almost ranch-like, nicely cuts through the charred kimchi. The great Keens Steakhouse, Matt's favorite spot for rib eye and mutton in NYC, butts up against Manhattan's Koreatown, so this could be a tribute to their geographical overlap as well.

1 cup matchstick-size thick-cut bacon, cut ¼ inch wide

2 wedges or quarters whole head kimchi (pogi)

1 bunch scallions, white and green parts, thinly sliced and soaked in ice water

2 tablespoons toasted sesame seeds

DRESSING

One 16-ounce package silken tofu

½ cup rice vinegar

2 tablespoons honey

2 tablespoons sesame oil

1 tablespoon kosher salt

1 Line a plate with paper towels and set it near the stove. Heat a dry medium skillet over medium heat. When the pan is hot, add the bacon and cook, stirring occasionally, until crispy, 7 to 10 minutes. Using a slotted spoon, transfer the bacon to the towel-lined plate to absorb any excess grease.

2 Prepare an outdoor grill (preferably charcoal) for direct cooking over high heat. Place the kimchi quarters over the fire and grill, turning once, until they have a good char but are still crisp, 2 to 3 minutes on each side. This step can also be done indoors using a cast-iron grill pan over high heat. Remove and let cool completely.

3 **Make the dressing:** In a medium bowl, whisk together all the ingredients until smooth. A blender will work great too. You should have about 2 cups dressing. You will not need it all for the salad, and the remainder will keep in an airtight container in the refrigerator for up to a month.

4 Arrange the kimchi on a platter and garnish with the scallions, bacon, and sesame seeds. Pour some of the dressing over the kimchi and serve.

Confessions of a Ten-Year-Old Kimchi Jjigae Super Fan

Jason Ough is Matt's Korean Best Friend (KBF), and he lives in the Bay Area with his wife, Jennie, and two amazing kids, Aerim and Andrew. Matt and Jason have been friends since college, and they spoke for an interview in *Koreatown* about Jason's two-year-old daughter, Aerim, being raised with Korean food in her life. (She was pictured in the book eating kalbi off the bone.) "She needs to know her heritage and where she comes from, or at least where her grandparents come from, anyway," her father said. Jason, good job. Your daughter is the best, and here she is eight years later, speaking for herself.

For *Koreatown,* we interviewed your dad and asked him about raising his two-year-old daughter, Aerim, around Korean food. Hey, that's you! What do you think about Korean food?

I think it's delicious, and I really like the spicy food. One of my favorites is kimchi jjigae. That's like tofu and pork belly, and it has lots of really good foods in it. Plus, I love rice. I love kimbap. It's like Korean sushi but with Spam in it. I really like Spam.

Do you make kimchi jjigae?

My grandma does. She makes it really, really good.

Do you crave Korean food?

Yes. It's so good. When my grandma makes kimchi jjigae and leaves it out, I can't help but start eating it. [Aerim's six-year-old brother, Andrew, jumps in: I like to eat it too.]

Back to kimbap. Do you help the adults make it?

Yes, it's really fun to make. There's a lot of cutting and prepping.

Do you eat Korean food at school?

When my grandma comes, she makes me kimbap, and I take it to school.

Are the kids jealous that the food is so good?

Yes!

Let's talk about your own cooking. Are there any Korean dishes that you make?

I've helped out with making different kinds of muk. It's clear, and you make it on the stove, and you have to mix it a lot, and then you let it cool, and you have to cut it into blocks like tofu and put a soy-saucy sauce on it.

What about Korean barbecue? In your dad's interview, he talked about getting you into Korean food, and we printed a photo of you eating kalbi off the bone. Do you still like kalbi?

I love kalbi because I really like meat, and it's just so good. I love the flavor.

Do you want to visit Korea one day?

Yes, I want to go there just to try all of the new foods. I want to try the kimchi and kalbi. I also love the Korean sweet potato called goguma. [Andrew: Ohhhh, I love goguma too!]

Q&A
WHY TWO-YEAR-OLDS NEED TO EAT KALBI

Jason Ough is Matt's Korean best friend (KBF) and, with his wife, Jennie, has raised quite possibly the cutest little girl in the Bay Area, which they call home. Matt and Jason were texting about the terribleness of the New York Knicks one day, when Jason slipped in a photo of his daughter Aerim eating kalbi off the bone. Whoa! It got Matt thinking that he needed to find out from Jason about what it's like raising a very young child on Korean food.

So, you just got your two-year-old daughter to eat kalbi off the bone! How proud are you?
We're pretty proud. She's got all of her teeth in now—finally—so she's able to really get in there and grind the meat down. We gave her one with the bone cut off, and she had a meltdown and demanded the full piece with the bone in. So we gave it to her. And she went to town on it.

Why is it important to cook Korean food for your daughter?
She needs to know her heritage and where she comes from. Or at least where her grandparents come from. We want her to know that it's important—the entire ceremony of preparing, serving, and eating it.

I grew up in Wisconsin. I didn't have a Korean community around me, so I never had that all-encompassing, 360-degree cultural experience. But I still had my mom, and she cooked us Korean food almost every single day. We'd drive to Chicago's Koreatown once a month to stock up and we'd keep it all in an old fridge on our back porch. It held the kimchi and other foods

that were too stinky to keep alongside our "white" foods, like 2 percent milk and Wonder bread. I even bought a six-pack mini-fridge in medical school and used that as a kimchi fridge in my apartment.

So that was largely the basis of my Korean identity while growing up: our food. That's why it's so important to me, and to my wife as well. And since we want to make sure that Aerim will embrace Korean food and culture, we make it a point to get her to try as much of it as possible, teaching her the proper names and everything. And we will always have a kimchi fridge.

But she's not really feeling kimchi yet?
Not yet. We'll get there. We've tried, but she just cries when she tastes anything spicy. She can barely handle the mild pico de gallo from the burrito shop down the street, so it may take some trying to work up to true Korean-caliber kimchi. But she will get there. She's Korean, she has to eat kimchi. It's in her blood. It's her destiny.

TED AND YONG KIM HAVE BIG PLANS FOR KOREAN BOXED LUNCH

"We could have easily called it a bento, but we had to represent Korean dosirak in its truest form." We are hanging out in the commissary kitchen of Seoul Sausage Company, a part prep space—part clubhouse located in an industrial patch of downtown Los Angeles, close to where the 110 and the 101 intertwine like spaghetti. Ted Kim, who founded the genuinely OG LA Korean catering and restaurant group with his brother, Yong, nearly a decade ago, has just overseen a large catering order for the Netflix offices and is taking a little break. We're talking about his booming boxed-lunch business, and how a no-compromise approach to the Korean-style cooking (and naming convention) has earned the company a strong reputation in the city with America's largest Korean diasporic population. But, he says, there's still a lot of work to be done in terms of breaking down stereotypes. "Even if it's harder, even if it's a little more confusing to some, it's better for us to talk about it. I do this to share my culture."

The COVID-19 pandemic was hard on all those working in restaurants, yet Ted and Yong were quick to spot an opportunity with their dosirak idea: boxed lunches packed with tidy compartments of bulgogi, kalbi sausages, mac salad made with Best Foods mayo, oi muchim (cucumber salad), and a small bundle of baechu (napa cabbage) kimchi, either picked up at a window or delivered to the offices of studios and fashion designers around Los Angeles.

Business has been growing steadily, with Netflix in particular becoming a regular customer. Is it just a coincidence, given the streaming company's strong investment (more than $700 million in 2023) in Korean-made shows, including hits like *Squid Game*, *Itaewon Class*, *Extraordinary Attorney Woo*, and *Kingdom*? "We once had a special order for kimbap with our sausages in it, and they wouldn't tell us if it was for any of the cast, but we also watched *Attorney Woo*," he says with a smile.

There is little coincidence between the growth of Seoul Sausage's Netflix business and the crescendo moment of Korean pop culture blowing up in the mainstream. The streaming service has invested big in Korean-made television and is only showing signs of bringing more Korean pop culture into homes across the world.

Ted and Yong are certainly no strangers to the collision of food and television. Competing in the reality TV arena, they took first place in season three of the Food Network's *The Great Food Truck Race* and second place in *The Great Food Truck Race: All Stars*. Offers come in frequently for television appearances by the personable brothers. "Bourdain already did all of that," Ted says of turning down offers. What gives the Kim brothers the most joy is not the ups and downs of food TV celebrity, but the mission to expand Korean food to a large audience. "We just want to put out the best dosirak possible. It's just lunch," he says with a pause and a smile. "It's Korean lunch."

KARAE JUMEOKBAP
CRISPY CURRY RICE BALLS
카래 주먹밥

MAKES 12 BALLS

Ted and Yong Kim of Seoul Sausage Company created this dish to honor their first food truck location on Sawtelle Boulevard (aka Japantown) on the Westside of Los Angeles. They knew they wanted to tackle the classic Japanese curry but incorporate it into crispy rice balls, which are traditionally made with kimchi. It's now a staple of their dosirak business. The recipe works with all types of rice, including medium grain, Calrose, and jasmine, but as the Kim brothers cooked these in the tight confines of a truck, they realized that instant rice worked best.

RICE BALLS

4 cups water

Kosher salt

2 cups instant rice (preferably Minute rice)

One 3.2-ounce box Japanese curry sauce mix (preferably S&B Golden Curry hot)

2 medium potatoes, peeled and cut into ½-inch cubes

2 tablespoons chopped fresh cilantro

Neutral cooking oil, for deep-frying

¼ cup all-purpose flour

2 eggs

1½ cups panko

SAUCE

1 cup Kewpie brand mayonnaise

2 tablespoons pickled ginger, finely chopped

1   **Make the rice balls:** In a small saucepan, combine 2 cups of the water and ½ teaspoon salt and bring to a boil over high heat. Add the rice, stir well, remove from the heat, and cover the pan. Let sit for 5 minutes, then transfer the rice to a medium bowl. Set aside.

2   Break up the curry sauce blocks, transfer to a small saucepan, and add the remaining 2 cups water. Bring to a boil over medium-high heat, lower the heat to a simmer, and cook, stirring periodically, until the curry dissolves and the sauce is very thick, about 10 minutes.

3   While the sauce is cooking, bring a medium saucepan filled with salted water to a boil. Add the potatoes and cook until just tender, 5 to 7 minutes. Be careful not to overcook them. Drain, rinse under cold running water, and then drain again. Make sure the potatoes are well drained before they are added to the rice.

4   Add the curry sauce to the rice and mix well. Add the potatoes and cilantro and mix again until evenly distributed. Season with salt if needed. Refrigerate the mixture, uncovered, until cool.

5   Using your palms, roll the cooled rice mixture into 3½-ounce balls (scant ½ cup each) and arrange on a plate. Return the balls, uncovered, to the refrigerator to cool down further and harden, about 1 hour.

6   Pour 2 inches of oil into a Dutch oven and heat over medium-high heat to 350°F.

7   While the oil heats, set up a breading station. Put the flour, eggs, and panko into three separate small bowls. Season the flour with a pinch of salt. Beat the eggs until blended. Dredge a rice ball in the flour, coating evenly and tapping off the excess. Next, roll it in the eggs, letting the excess drip off. Finally, roll it in the panko, coating evenly. Set aside on a plate. Repeat with the remaining balls.

8   Working in batches, add the balls to the hot oil and fry, turning occasionally, until golden brown, crispy, and heated through, 5 to 7 minutes. Using tongs, transfer to a paper towel–lined plate.

9   **Make the sauce:** Stir together the mayonnaise and ginger and drizzle over the rice balls.

TANGSUYUK VIA DONGBEI GUO BAO ROU
SWEET-AND-SOUR PORK
탕수육

SERVES 2

Lucas Sin is a Hong Kong–born, US-educated chef and social media creator, and he's behind some of the biggest ideas in home and restaurant cooking. (You should definitely catch him on Instagram for his cooking videos and, more important, for his razor-sharp commentary on food culture.) Today, Sin is roaming Asia as he researches future recipes. He's splitting his time between Hong Kong and Shanghai while visiting places like Seoul for extended periods.

Sweet-and-sour pork, called tangsuyuk, is one of the great Korean-Chinese dishes, which are Korean spins on classics from their larger neighbor. We wanted to get Sin's take on tangsuyuk, which is presented here as Chinese dongbei guo bao rou – the source material for Korean tangsuyuk. It's a bit circular, we admit, but the recipe is worth it. As for the difference between the two dishes? We combed historical archives and spoke with chefs in the United States and Korea, and eventually with Sin, and the consensus was that tangsuyuk is usually tossed with vegetables like wood ear mushrooms, onions, and carrots. This recipe is absolutely one of our favorites.

SWEET-AND-SOUR SAUCE

1 cup sugar

1 cup distilled white vinegar

2 tablespoons fresh lemon juice

8 ounces boneless pork shoulder, thinly sliced against the grain

1½ teaspoons kosher salt

Pinch of ground white pepper

1 tablespoon Shaoxing wine

1 cup potato starch

3 cups water

Neutral cooking oil, for cooking

4 garlic cloves, thinly sliced lengthwise

½-inch knob fresh ginger, cut into very thin 2-inch strips

¼ cup cut-up cilantro stems, in 2-inch lengths

3 scallions, white part only, cut into very thin 2-inch-long strips

1 **Make the sauce:** In a small, heavy saucepan, combine the sugar and vinegar and bring to a boil over medium heat. There is no need to stir. Continue to boil until most of the harsh vinegar flavor has evaporated, 2 to 4 minutes. Continue to cook until slightly reduced and the flavor is a mellow, balanced sweet-and-sour, about 2 minutes longer. Remove from the heat and stir in the lemon juice. Let cool, cover, and chill in the refrigerator.

2 Using a mallet or the back of a knife, hammer each pork slice to tenderize the meat until it is almost double in size and half its original thickness. If needed, cut the pounded slices into smaller pieces about 1½ inches square.

3 In a medium bowl, combine the pork, salt, pepper, and wine and mix thoroughly with your hands, squeezing the seasoning into the meat. Cover and refrigerate for at least 30 minutes or up to 3 days.

4 In a large metal bowl, combine the potato starch and water and stir together until fully mixed and a thick paste forms. Leave the bowl on the counter for 30 minutes, at which point the water and the starch will have separated again. Pour off the excess water and keep the remaining paste-like substance. (If you or your kids have played with oobleck, you know what this is. Yes, it's edible!)

5 Gradually add the starch batter to the pork, massaging it into the meat until a thin coating of batter barely covers each piece and you can only faintly see the pink of the meat. The batter should be difficult to move through, but it will run off when stationary. Add 1 tablespoon oil and mix well.

6   In a wok or Dutch oven, heat ½ cup oil over medium-high heat to 300°F. Adjust the heat as necessary to maintain the temperature. Carefully drop the pork slices into the hot oil and fry until they are flat and set in shape, about 2 minutes. Transfer to a plate.

7   Raise the oil temperature to 375°F. Return the pork slices to the oil and fry for 1 minute to finish cooking. Transfer the pork to the same plate.

8   Finally, raise the oil temperature to 400°F. Add the pork slices and fry one more time for a deeper golden shade, about 30 seconds. Remove the oil from the heat. If you used a wok for the frying steps, carefully pour off the oil into a heatproof container and wipe out the pan to use for the final step.

9   Heat 2 tablespoons oil over medium-high heat until it shimmers. Add the garlic and ginger and stir-fry until aromatic, about 30 seconds. Add about ½ cup of the prepared sauce, mixing vigorously until bubbles appear and the sauce thickens slightly. Add the fried pork, cilantro stems, and scallions and toss to combine. Transfer to a serving dish and serve warm.

JJOLMYEON
SWEET HEAT NOODLE SALAD
쫄면

SERVES 4

Stella Pak is the creative brain behind Noona Noodles, one of our favorite Korean noodle shops in New York City. Pak, a former magazine beauty editor (one of the cool ones), launched Noona (translation: "big sister") in the busy Food Gallery 32 food court in the heart of Manhattan's Koreatown in 2018, and she hasn't looked back. Working with her mother, Byung-Sul Kim, Pak is helping pioneer the next generation of NYC's Koreatown. While the noodles sold at Noona are versions of the classics like sujebi (dough flakes), jjamppong (wheat noodles in seafood broth), and ramyun, they are presented with an eye for bold flavors, possible internet viral takeoff in their naming (check the Frat Boy Ramen), and full deliciousness. We've taken many hard-core Korean food fans to Noona, and they've been blown away by Pak's menu of noodles.

When we started talking to Pak about a recipe, we were taken back to her now-closed Hi Noona restaurant in the East Village. Walking in, you were greeted by a lineup of Korean wellness drinks and salads. We were instantly like, "Whoa, here's the Korean Sweetgreen we've always hoped for." Crisp salads with toasted rice, vegan mushroom bowls with kim, and smoothies made with the homeopathic multigrain powder misugaru. One of her items from that menu remains stuck in our heads. Jjolmyeon (chewy noodles) is as much a salad as a noodle dish, with crunchy julienned vegetables and hard-boiled eggs sitting on top of chilled wheat noodles. The "sweet heat" in the name is a tip to the sauce, which includes a full-bodied puree of pineapple followed by the heat from chile. If you cannot find jjolmyeon, substitute buckwheat noodles.

1 pound dried jjolmyeon noodles

1 cup soybean sprouts

Kosher salt

Sesame oil, for drizzling

½ cup peeled, julienned carrots

½ seedless cucumber, julienned

1 cup shredded purple or green cabbage

2 hard-boiled eggs, peeled and halved lengthwise

Sesame seeds, for garnish

DRESSING

1 tablespoon gochugaru

1 tablespoon gochujang

1 tablespoon honey

1½ teaspoons soy sauce

1 tablespoon rice vinegar

1 tablespoon sesame oil

1½ teaspoons sesame seeds

¼ cup cubed, canned or fresh pineapple (drained if canned)

1 garlic clove, minced

1   Bring a large pot of water to a boil over high heat. Add the noodles and cook according to the package instructions. Make sure to stir frequently so they do not stick together. The noodles should be desirably chewy. Using tongs, lift the noodles out of the pot and drop them into a colander, then rinse under cold running water and set aside, keeping the boiling water on the stove.

2   Add the bean sprouts to the boiling water and blanch for 2 minutes. Drain and rinse under cold running water. Dry well and season with salt and a drizzle of oil. Set aside to bring to room temperature.

3   **Make the dressing:** In a food processor, combine all the ingredients and process until well mixed. The pineapple can remain a little chunky, which gives the noodles bursts of brightness. The dressing can be made up to 1 week ahead and stored in an airtight container in the refrigerator.

4   To assemble, divide the cold noodles among four bowls. Top with the bean sprouts, carrots, cucumber, and cabbage. Top each bowl with a dollop of dressing (at least 1 tablespoon and more if desired). Place a hard-boiled egg half at the center of each bowl and drizzle with oil. Garnish with sesame seeds and serve.

KOREAN GROCERY 2.0 STARTS WITH QUEENS, AN ONLINE SUPERETTE WITH BIG PLANS

When it comes to food, San Francisco has arguably the most captive, excited, supportive, and oftentimes opinionated population in the United States. Restaurants thrive and fade away like seasonal citrus, and SF can be a pretty tough place to hack it as an operator. Deuki, who operates restaurants in the city, certainly has his thoughts about the environment. It's hard to pinpoint exactly why Bay Area Korean restaurants haven't been given the national spotlight and, in some cases, even the local respect they deserve.

Yet since the summer of 2019, former education and tech executives Eddo Kim and Clara Lee have been changing the perception of Korean restaurants and grocery stores by running Queens in the city's Inner Sunset neighborhood. "It's not authentic, it's not fusion, and, in a lot of ways, what we are doing is not linear," Lee says. "There are, of course, foundational ingredients and elements of Korean food and cooking, and there needs to be respect given to them. But when we put a tomato kimchi or a fennel geotjeori (fresh kimchi) on the menu and people say we are cooking fusion, it's maybe not the right term." Indeed, the cooking at Queens is original, yet in some ways it could be right at home in contemporary Korea. *Was* original. Sadly, Queens closed its storefront in July 2023, just as we were wrapping up this book. This is not the end of a story but a new beginning, as Queens establishes its grocery presence online and evolves with the times.

While sitting in their sunny dining room for an interview, we're treated to an avalanche of dishes they serve from a menu that covers many of the modern hits we discussed earlier in the book: cooking that observes the leading-edge food being made in Seoul and Busan while still being grounded in the States. There's an overstuffed and eggy gilgeori toast (see page 43) made with Cheddar cheese and raspberry jam, and a namul bap prepared with seasoned chrysanthemum. Queens has earned a reputation for jeon, and during our extensive travels, we could not find a better version in the United States, especially its haemul buchupajeon (page 191). Shrimp, cuttlefish, and plenty of vegetables (garlic chives, zucchini, Fresno chile) come together in a crispy pancake that has earned Kim and Lee legendary status, at least in our book. (You can buy their pancake mix online.)

This leads to the retail superette part of Queens. "We are a little different from H Mart," Kim says, crediting her customers for valuing small businesses and supporting Korean craftsmanship. This is by no means a shot at the largest retailer of Korean foods in the United States, but more a clear effort to shift the way Korean American–led retail can operate on a smaller level—sourcing from local producers and merchandizing the store more like a curated specialty foods shop than a supermarket. It's a sign of exciting retail opportunities to come.

"We have such a bounty here in California, so we're making our mushroom salt with some of the best Northern California mushrooms," says Lee. She notes that the Queens line of products (pancake mix, gochugaru, salt) is available at more than twenty-five retailers around the country. "We can do it ourselves in many ways, and we're small and mobile, and it's one of our greatest strengths." Another strength: that salt on *that* pancake.

HAEMUL BUCHUPAJEON
SEAFOOD AND GARLIC CHIVE PANCAKE
해물부추파전

MAKES 1 EXTRA-LARGE PANCAKE

At Queens in San Francisco, owners Eddo Kim and Clara Lee perfected the art of the Korean pancake — not just aesthetically (it's gorgeous) but also flavor-wise. At the restaurant that was open until summer 2023, they infused their frying oil with garlic chives and other alliums, which give the pancake an added depth of flavor (see Note). And they keep all the ingredients very cold until the pancake comes in contact with the hot oil to ensure the batter will contract quickly and create a crisp base crust and surface. The batter is kept very minimal so the other ingredients (alliums and seafood) are the stars of the dish. You can buy Queens's incredible pancake mix online (visit queenssf.com) or use your favorite brand.

Note: While it's not necessary, if you'd like to do the Queens infused-oil trick, here's how: In a small saucepan, combine 2 to 3 cups neutral cooking oil with 12 garlic cloves, thinly sliced lengthwise; 1 bunch garlic chives, chopped; 1 white onion, sliced; or a combination of any other alliums you may have on hand. Bring to a simmer over low heat and simmer for 2 hours. Let sit at room temperature for 2 days, then strain, bottle, and cap tightly. The oil will keep in the fridge for several months.

¾ cup Korean pancake mix

½ cup water, Anchovy Stock (page 47), or stock of your choice

1 egg

4 ounces large shrimp, shelled and cleaned

4 ounces cuttlefish, cleaned (optional)

2 cups cut-up fresh garlic chives, in 2-inch lengths

1 cup matchstick-size zucchini, in 1-inch lengths

½ cup thinly sliced yellow onion

½ cup thinly sliced Korean chile

¼ cup neutral or allium-infused cooking oil

1   In a medium bowl, whisk together the pancake mix, water, and egg until smooth. Cover and refrigerate until ready to cook.

2   Cut the shrimp and cuttlefish (if using) into bite-size pieces. Bring a small saucepan filled with water to a boil over high heat. Add the seafood and blanch for 2 minutes. Drain, rinse under cold running water, and transfer to a small bowl. Cover and refrigerate until ready to use.

3   When ready to cook, add the seafood, garlic chives, zucchini, onion, and chile to the batter and mix thoroughly. In a large skillet (at least 12 inches in diameter), heat the oil over high heat until it shimmers. Carefully drop the batter into the hot oil by spoonfuls and then, using the back of a spoon, spread it out until the pancake is about 10 inches in diameter. Fry until a golden brown crust forms on the bottom, 2 to 3 minutes. Lower the heat to medium, flip the pancake, and fry until the second side is golden brown, 2 to 3 minutes longer. Transfer to a serving plate and serve hot.

Adoption, Adaption, and Korean American Food through an Alternative Lens

New York City chef Kate Telfeyan was born in Korea and adopted in 1982 by parents living in rural Rhode Island, where she was raised. After college and stints in book publishing and in public relations for a catering company she started, Telfeyan moved to New York to pursue "either food or book publishing or both." She worked at Simon & Schuster before switching to full-time work first at a catering company, then in public relations, and eventually on the line, serving as head chef at Mission Chinese Food and later opening her own restaurant, Porcelain, in Ridgewood, Queens, which was very well reviewed and operated until summer 2023.

What was food like growing up? "My mom was a great cook. And an instinctual cook. Nothing was very fancy, but it was always very good and very satisfying," she says. And what about Korean food? "Nope." She laughs. "The first time I had Korean food was when I was a senior in high school, and my mom took me to a place that had opened in Providence. Neither of us had any idea what we were doing. I remember thinking, 'It's fine.' [Laughs.] My first introduction to Asian food, like for a lot of people, was suburban Chinese food."

As Telfeyan's experience with cooking Korean food grew, it was fun to watch the menu at Porcelain change over time. Korean-inspired dishes landed with frequency, including a kimchi-brined fried chicken and gyeranjjim (steamed egg), with the restaurant's version served with chile granola and scallion oil. The granola was the chef's homage to the salty snacks of her youth (Chex Mix and Gardetto's were favorites). The mixture featured roasted redskin peanuts tossed in dry spices and chile oil, then combined with fried shallots, fried garlic, and toasted sesame seeds.

Telfeyan also served braised oxtails that were loosely inspired by the bubbling sokkoritang (oxtail soup), presenting the oxtails with a small amount of the braising liquid and fermented radish stem and with three individual condiment ramekins—one containing gochugaru and salt, one of chonggak (ponytail radish) kimchi, and one with shredded ginger and soy sauce.

The future is bright for the young cook, and Telfeyan's approach represents that of a swelling number of Korean adoptee chefs exploring their roots within the American restaurant scene.

"There's so much history of Korean families opening restaurants and changing the culture of Southern California, and we didn't want to fuck with that. That isn't our story to tell," says John Hong. We're sitting in the dining room of Yangban, a sprawling former French bistro located across from Warner Music Group in a previously industrial, now trendy stretch of downtown Los Angeles. It's midafternoon, a few hours before service is set to begin, and John and his wife and partner, Katianna Hong, have sat down to tell us the story that they *do* have to tell. It's the story of the next generation of Korean American cooking in Los Angeles—the children of the established Koreatown that "have a little more room to create and be exploratory in their endeavors," in a city that has, in the past half decade, embraced a clutch of more progressive Korean American restaurants, with Yangban leading the charge.

The duo's backgrounds lend themselves well to this exploration. John grew up in a predominantly Jewish suburb of Chicago, while Katianna was adopted by a Jewish couple and was raised in upstate New York. They would go on to cook at some of the most decorated restaurants in America, including Alinea in Chicago; Meadowood in Napa Valley, where Katianna was named chef de cuisine in 2015; and Mélisse in Los Angeles. But it's been Yangban that has earned the duo wide acclaim from both food editors and the James Beard Foundation, which put the restaurant on the list of the best new restaurants in America in 2023.

The crossover of Korean and Jewish cooking is fully on display at Yangban, which was originally conceived to run like a Jewish deli at lunchtime, with a point-and-grab glass counter placed in the center of the space. As for the menu, there's a matzo ball soup with hand-torn dough flakes (sujebi) replacing the matzo (Katianna's Jewish grandmother's recipe), a Korean latke with squash replacing potatoes (see pictured, opposite), and a soondae-style bratwurst with white kimchi kraut.

Deuki asks if the pair considers Yangban a Korean restaurant, which is the same question I ask Kate about Porcelain, and the same question that we've brought up to acclaimed Madison, Wisconsin, chef Tory Miller of the legendary, French-inspired landmark L'Etoile (see page 224), another Korean adoptee who has found his own voice while negotiating his multiple identities. This group of adopted Korean chefs is also joined by Philadelphia's Peter Serpico, a former Momofuku boss who would go on to write about his own journey in the book *Learning Korean*, and Danny Bowien, the Oklahoma-raised, New York City–based prodigy who is continuing his journey to fuse fashion, downtown nightlife, and food in the most exciting ways.

It's a tough question to answer. "We started as a Korean-Jewish deli in the middle of the pandemic. It was ambitious, it was large, and over the course of time since opening, we have evolved," says Katianna. At the press deadline of this book, the Los Angeles chefs were still working through a way to sustain their ambitious plans. But back to Deuki's question: Is it a Korean restaurant? If you ask the fans of Miller, Serpico, Bowien, Telfeyan, and the chefs of Yangban— along with the thousands of other adopted professionals working in food—the answer is, of course, yes. If you've made it this far in the book, Korean food today cares little about borders and even less about labels.

FAMILY MEAL KIMCHI JJIGAE
엄마 김치찌개

SERVES 3 OR 4

Kate Telfeyan was the chef-partner of Porcelain, a New York City restaurant serving truly delicious Korean American cooking, like kimchi-brined fried chicken and loaded ssamjang vegetable platters, along with dishes inspired by Sichuan, China, and other parts of Asia. (She calls it "vaguely Asian.") Over the years, as a chef working in kitchens like Mission Chinese Food, Telfeyan has done her version of kimchi jjigae for the staff meal before service. It's a stew that, by Telfeyan's account, varies slightly from more traditional iterations but has evolved over many years of experimentation, often based on what was available at whatever kitchen she was working in at the time. This version incorporates Shin Ramyun (Korean instant noodle soup), rice cakes, and chopped kimchi and its liquid. As with all kimchi jjigae, the liquid from the chopped kimchi is gold and should be incorporated into the bubbling broth.

"In the absence of pork belly, I've been known to throw in some deli ham or even mortadella scraps, and no one version was ever better than another. They all inspired the same emotional and gustatory response," she says. "For me, the number one rule for making something satisfying and delicious is a lot like the expression 'dance as if no one is watching'—make it personal, be expressive, and have fun."

2 tablespoons neutral cooking oil

2 garlic cloves, chopped

½ cup gochujang

1-inch knob fresh ginger, grated

8 ounces skinless pork belly, thinly sliced

4 cups chopped kimchi, with liquid reserved (½ to 1 cup)

⅓ cup gochugaru

1 cup Kombu Stock (recipe follows)

2 packages spicy instant Korean beef ramen (such as Shin Ramyun), including the soup base packets (optional)

1 teaspoon sugar

1 teaspoon ground black pepper

1 teaspoon soy sauce

½ cup fish sauce

One 16-ounce package silken tofu

3 cups sliced rice cakes (the type used for soup)

1 bunch scallions, white and green parts, cut into 2-inch lengths with white and green kept separate

1 medium onion, sliced

½ teaspoon sesame oil

Toasted sesame seeds, for garnish

1   In a Dutch oven or other large, heavy pot, heat the neutral oil over medium-high heat until it shimmers. Add the garlic, gochujang, and ginger and sauté until aromatic, 2 to 3 minutes.

2   Add the pork belly and cook, stirring occasionally, about 2 minutes. Add the chopped kimchi and cook, stirring occasionally, until aromatic, about 2 minutes longer. Add the gochugaru and stir to mix well.

3   Pour in the stock and kimchi liquid and add the soup base packets (if using). Let the stew come to a boil, then turn down the heat to a simmer and simmer for 5 minutes. Add the sugar, pepper, soy sauce, and fish sauce and stir well.

4   Using a large soup spoon or dinner spoon, scoop out the tofu in chunks and add to the stew (or you can cube it and add it). Raise the heat to medium-high and return the stew to a boil. Add the rice cakes, ramen noodles, scallion whites, and onion and boil until the noodles are cooked, about 5 minutes.

5   Add the scallion greens and stir. Finish with the sesame oil, garnish with sesame seeds, and serve.

Kombu Stock
다시마 육수]

MAKES ABOUT 6 CUPS

8 cups water

Eight 5-inch squares kombu (dashima)

8 dried shiitake mushrooms

1   In a large saucepan, combine the water, kombu, and mushrooms and bring to a boil over medium-high heat. Turn down the heat to low and simmer, uncovered, for 20 minutes.

2   Remove from the heat, remove the kombu and mushrooms, and discard the kombu. You can discard the mushrooms as well, or you can stem them, slice the caps, and add them to the stew with the tofu. Use the stock immediately, or let cool, transfer to an airtight container, and store in the refrigerator for up to a week.

Rice Water
쌀뜨물

MAKES 6 CUPS

1 cup rice (any kind), unrinsed

9 cups water

This is one of the standard hacks to lean on when cooking anything from a jjigae or a tang to sauces and braises. If a recipe calls for anchovy- or vegetable-based stock, but you don't have time to make it, you are still in luck. When rinsing rice, a necessary step before cooking nearly any grain, home cooks often throw away the water. But that cloudy liquid is actually perfect for using as part of the base for a soup or stew. Its rice flavor gives your dishes a little more taste than the standard pipe stock (aka hot water).

1   In a medium bowl, combine the rice and 3 cups of the water and swirl the rice in the water with your fingers to rinse it.

2   Drain the rice and discard the first batch of water, as it is too starchy.

3   Add 3 cups of the water to the rice and again rinse the rice thoroughly by swirling it in the water.

4   Drain the rice, this time capturing the water in a second medium bowl. Return the rice to its bowl.

5   Add the remaining 3 cups water to the rice and again rinse the rice thoroughly by swirling it in the water. Drain the rice, capturing the water in the bowl holding the previous batch of rinsing water. You now have 6 cups of rice water perfect for enriching stews, soups, and other dishes.

HONEY BUTTER CORN RIBS
허니버터 옥수수

SERVES 4 TO 6

When Mission Chinese Food opened in New York in a crowded, subterranean space on Orchard Street over a decade ago, the food world collectively paused to praise the inventive and fully out-there Chinese cooking of a young Korean American chef named Danny Bowien. An adoptee raised by a white family in Oklahoma, his food was inspired by equal parts Chinese American takeout, food he tasted in China, and his own galaxy-wandering brain. Over the years, though, he found a new voice for himself while diving into Korean cooking.

Corn ribs are corn on the cob cut to resemble baby back ribs. The salty-sweet sauce is based on the butter-corn craze that "hit Korea some years back, when the company Haitai released a very tasty honey butter variety of potato chips that caused more hype in Seoul than a Supreme drop in SoHo," says Bowien.

The XXX spice mix is the kicker here, with the mouth-numbing effect of the green Sichuan peppercorns keeping the sweetness in check while its warm spices, clove and cardamom, take that sweetness in an unexpected direction.

1   **Make the spice mix:** In a spice grinder or coffee grinder, combine all the ingredients and grind to a fine powder. Transfer to an airtight container. Depending on the size of your grinder, you may need to do this in batches; once all the batches are ground, stir together well. You will need only ¼ cup for the corn ribs. The remainder will keep in the pantry for up to 2 months before it starts to lose its vibrancy.

2   **Make the corn ribs:** Position one rack in the center and the other in the upper third of the oven and preheat the oven to 350ºF.

3   Using a heavy, sharp knife, cut each corn ear in half crosswise, then quarter each half lengthwise through the cob. Trim away most of the cob on each quarter, leaving ½ inch.

4   In a large bowl, combine the corn ribs and ¼ cup of the oil and toss to coat well. Sprinkle the spice mix, salt, and pepper over the corn and toss to coat evenly. Spread the corn in a single layer on two large sheet pans. Bake the corn, switching the pans between the racks and rotating from back to front halfway through baking, until the corn curls and browns, 15 to 20 minutes.

5   While the corn bakes, in a wok or small skillet, combine the butter, garlic, and the remaining 2 tablespoons oil. Place over medium-high heat and let the butter melt and the fat sizzle. Cook until the garlic is golden brown, about 1 minute. Remove from the heat, stir in the soy sauce and agave syrup, and cover to keep warm.

6   When the corn ribs are ready, transfer to a large platter, drizzle with the butter sauce, and garnish with seaweed.

XXX SPICE MIX

2 tablespoons whole cloves

2 tablespoons fennel seeds

2 tablespoons green Sichuan peppercorns

2 tablespoons green cardamom pods

2 tablespoons shiitake mushroom powder

2 tablespoons sugar

2 tablespoons cayenne pepper

CORN RIBS

6 ears corn, husked

¼ cup plus 2 tablespoons extra-virgin olive oil

¼ cup XXX Spice Mix

½ teaspoon kosher salt

½ teaspoon ground black pepper

4 tablespoons unsalted butter (vegan butter if going with Bowien's plant-based vibe)

2 tablespoons thinly sliced garlic

2 tablespoons soy sauce

1 tablespoon agave syrup, maple syrup, or honey

1 tablespoon shredded roasted nori seaweed (kim), for garnish

MODERN RICE:

THE LONG AND SHORT

OF IT ALL

A trip to the rice aisle of any Asian grocery store will present you with many choices. First, there's place of origin: Korea, India, China, Thailand, Sri Lanka, the United States. There is grain size: short, medium, long. Then there are the varieties, with some forty thousand in existence. Colusa vs. Bhut Muri vs. Red Cargo, anyone? Rice is a critical ingredient in the Korean kitchen, and in many cases, a meal isn't a meal without it. Yet Korean rice culture goes so much further than the palm-size metal bowl you will find nearly universally at Korean restaurants of all stripes. We love to eat rice in all forms—and we were so excited to find rice as the basis for creative and delicious new dishes all over the country.

In the chapter that follows, there's a bowl of juk (rice porridge) inspired by a favorite restaurant of chef Danny Lee in Northern Virginia and two ways to roll rice thanks to kimbap Basquiat Eunjo Park. There's a pineapple kimchi bokkeumbap (fried rice), because why not? And there's a bibimbap inspired by late-night fast food. Finally, Portland chef Peter Cho shows us how to use up the end of a soup or stew with butter, a little extra broth . . . and, of course, rice. We hope you enjoy this little detour into a small grain with a big personality.

HOW TO WASH AND COOK RICE

SERVES 4

Before we get into the wide world of creative rice dishes, it's always worth revisiting how to nail the basics. This is why we want to show you how to cook rice on the stove top. Of course, there are great electric rice cookers available, and most Korean families use them, but we're not going to assume that everyone has made the investment.

    A couple of things to keep in mind: Koreans stick with a short or medium grain. (The shorter the grain, the stickier the rice.) And before cooking the rice, you must properly rinse it. This is a step that can be forgotten, but it's crucial in removing the extra starches, the first step to avoiding gluey rice. It is also how you make rice water, which is a key component for adding flavor and thickening soups and stews (see page 199).

2 cups medium- or short-grain rice

2½ cups water

1   Place the rice in a large bowl. Run plenty of cold water over it, moving your fingers through the grains like you're scratching the head of a kitten. The liquid will turn cloudy. Tilt the bowl and discard the first batch of rice water down the drain. Repeat two or three times until the water runs visibly clearer. If you like, reserve these passes of rice water for thickening soups and stews (see page 199). Drain the rice (it is fine if there is a little residual water left over with the washed rice).

2   In a wide, medium saucepan or stone bowl, combine the rice and water. Koreans have a long tradition of cooking without measurements, known as son-mat (translation: the taste of one's hands, or using your own senses for judgment). To measure water this way, place your hand flat on top of the rice and allow the water to fill until it covers up to the spot where your fingers and palm meet, just at the start of your knuckle.

3   Set the pan aside for 30 minutes. The rice will absorb some of the water and return to room temperature.

4   Place the pan over high heat and bring the rice to a full boil. Drop the heat to a simmer over very low heat (an occasional bubble is okay), cover, and cook for 10 minutes. Take the pan completely off the heat and allow it to sit, covered, for an additional 10 minutes before serving. The cooked rice should be sticky, but you should be able to discern the individual grains.

Order #: 64

NORTHERN VIRGINIA DAKJUK

닭죽

SERVES 4

Juk Story, a seller of rice porridge, operates within the larger Siroo café in Annandale, Virginia, and sells juk in an eye-popping twenty-seven ways. This rice porridge (aka congee), or *juk* in Cantonese, is comforting and restorative. It's "mushy" for mush lovers and "creamy" for everyone else. At Juk Story, you'll find classic vegetable and less-classic tuna vegetable. There are riffs that merge the land and sea (oyster and mushroom) and a spicy bulgogi octopus that almost tempted us to go off our typically milder script. It's the Baskin-Robbins of porridge, and during a visit there with chef Danny Lee and his extremely cool mother, Yesoon (see page 162), we settled into our plan: spicy kimchi, abalone, and a play on the fortifying chicken-and-rice soup samgyetang, which inspired this recipe. We love how easy this dish comes together, and it's a great way to use up any leftover rotisserie chicken you have been puzzling over. Season to taste at the table with additional soy sauce and sesame oil, and toss in a few jujubes for color too.

1 cup short-grain rice

2 tablespoons sesame oil

2 garlic cloves, minced

1-inch knob fresh ginger, peeled and grated

½ cup whole bunapi (beech) mushrooms

½ cup peeled, finely diced carrot

½ cup finely diced onion

½ cup finely diced zucchini

Kosher salt and ground black pepper

6 cups chicken stock or Anchovy Stock (page 47)

2 to 3 cups pulled cooked chicken (dark and white meat)

1 large sheet roasted nori seaweed (kim), cut into thin strips

1 teaspoon toasted sesame seeds

2 dried jujubes, rehydrated and thinly sliced (optional)

Soy sauce, for serving

1   In a medium bowl, soak the rice in cold water to cover for 1 hour. Drain well.

2   In a medium, heavy saucepan, heat 1 tablespoon of the oil over high heat until it is lightly smoking. Add the garlic, ginger, and mushrooms and sauté until fragrant, about 30 seconds. Add the carrot, onion, and zucchini and sauté until the onion is translucent, about 3 minutes. Season with salt and pepper.

3   Add the drained rice and the remaining 1 tablespoon oil and toast lightly, stirring, for 1 minute.

4   Pour in the stock and bring to a boil. Drop the heat to a simmer and cook uncovered, stirring occasionally, until the mixture has taken on a porridge-like consistency, about 15 minutes. (Feel free to go on if you like the rice softer and the juk thicker.) Add the chicken at the last minute and simmer just until heated through, about 2 minutes. Season with salt and pepper.

5   Divide the juk among four bowls and garnish with the seaweed and sesame seeds. If you like, add the jujubes for color and to show your love for samgyetang. Serve with the soy sauce on the side.

EUNJO PARK'S KIMBAP WORLD TAKEOVER

Eunjo Park doesn't necessarily need kimbap, but kimbap most certainly needs her—or, at least, fans of kimbap need her. The traditional rolled-and-sliced snack is the marriage of kim (crisp sheets of roasted seaweed), seasoned rice, often a protein (such as tuna, beef, imitation crab, or … foie gras), and fresh or pickled vegetables, and it's Korea's answer to the Japanese nori roll. But kimbap is not "Korean sushi." It's its own unique (and some say superior) food group.

When chef Eunjo Park, a veteran of three Michelin-starred restaurants (Per Se and Momofuku Ko in New York and Gaon in Seoul), was opening the first Momofuku restaurant to focus explicitly on Korean food, Momofuku Kāwi, located in Manhattan's Hudson Yards, one of the very first dishes she and her boss, David Chang, wanted to feature was kimbap. "Dave came to me and asked what I think about kimbap, and I honestly wasn't sure how people could see it as something other than sushi, and how we could go beyond the traditional styles," she recalls. "It took me a while to break free, but once I did, I was having so much fun." Park's versions of kimbap exploded onto the New York dining scene, earning high praise, including from *New York Times* restaurant critic Pete Wells, who wrote in his rave review, "Kawi, from Momofuku, Takes Korean Food Head On," about Park's invention:

> Most kimbap is designed to be portable, filling and inexpensive. Ms. Park's kimbap, on the other hand, is built for pleasure. She has a pickled vegetable kimbap on the lunch menu that is truly exciting…. The dinner menu brings kimbap filled with chives, pickled daikon, citrus jelly and a buttery pink vein of foie gras terrine. Has this really never been done before, you wonder as you eat it, and if not, why not?

Why not? This was certainly Park's mindset when she and Chang decided to cure foie gras with a house seasoning salt that would become one of the restaurant's signatures and will likely follow her to future restaurants. Kāwi was forced to close during the COVID pandemic, and after working at sister restaurant Momofuku Ssäm Bar for a time, Park left Momofuku in September 2021 to focus on her own creative projects. Is there a solo kimbap project in the works? "Most definitely, that is something I would do," she says with a massive smile.

While writing this book, we talked to Park about working together on a couple of kimbap recipes (see page 211), and when we showed up at her Upper West Side apartment, she was ready for us with a tray of pickled carrots and peppers, seasoned rice, chives, mint, sautéed pea shoots, and a perfectly rolled omelet that mere cooking civilians would bat zero for twenty-five when attempting.

The setup of Park's kitchen is impressive and very chef soigné. We asked if there are ways to pare down the labor-intensive cooking, seasoning, rolling, and cutting that kimbap requires. First, know that you don't have to be a professional chef to make it, and your eggs certainly don't have be as perfectly rolled as hers. Buy as much as you can to save time, she says, suggesting we use store-bought versions of things like pickled radish (danmuji) and even shredded carrots. Then it's only a matter of roll, cut, and repeat to have a party's worth of kimbap on your table in no time. We hope you make these recipes or use them as a guide for future kimbap parties at home.

WANDUKONG KIMBAP
CHARRED PEA SHOOT KIMBAP
완두콩김밥

MAKES 2 ROLLS; SERVES 1

Making kimbap at home is one of those things that, to some, feels unreachable, illogical, and highly questionable — especially with so many great options available for sale in your local Koreatown and beyond. There is no getting around the fact that, for novices, rolling tight logs of seasoned rice and various cooked and raw components in seaweed requires a level of planning, a little patience, and a bamboo rolling mat — you know, the ones you've seen at your favorite kimbap or sushi counter. All disclaimers aside, this vegetable-based recipe from kimbap roller elite Eunjo Park is amazing and a great place to start. It's extremely fun to execute for a solo dinner project or to multiply the recipe for a party. Just give yourself some time for prep and practice.

Charring pea shoots (or baby spinach, baby kale, or other tender greens) gives the roll a distinct freshness and depth, while adding egg, chives, and pickled jalapeño brings in some classic kimbap flavors. A brush of sesame oil delivers a lasting burst of richness and is a key difference between Japanese maki and Korean kimbap.

OMELET
2 eggs

1 tablespoon extra-virgin olive oil

PEA SHOOTS
2 handfuls pea shoots, baby spinach, or baby kale

½ teaspoon extra-virgin olive oil

Kosher salt and ground black pepper

1 teaspoon sesame oil

Two 6-inch roasted sheets nori seaweed (kim)

1 cup Kimbap Rice (recipe follows)

½ cup drained Pickled Jalapeño (recipe follows)

1 bunch chives

½ medium carrot, peeled and julienned

8 fresh mint leaves

1 **Make the omelet:** In a small bowl, whisk the eggs until blended. In a small skillet, heat the olive oil over low heat. The pan should not be too hot or the delicate eggs will overcook. Pour the whisked eggs into the pan, swirl the pan to coat the bottom evenly, and cook until the eggs are set, about 2 minutes. Once they are set, holding an offset spatula in each hand, carefully roll the egg toward your body until you have a thick, rolled omelet log. Transfer to a plate and allow to cool for a couple of minutes.

2 **Make the pea shoots:** Heat a medium sauté pan over high heat until it is lightly smoking. Add the pea shoots, drizzle with the olive oil, and sprinkle with salt. Let the pea shoots sear, undisturbed, until charred, 1 minute or less. Toss quickly to make sure the greens are cooked until just tender. Transfer to a bowl, add the sesame oil, season with salt and pepper, and toss well. Cover and refrigerate until cooled.

3 **Assemble the kimbap:** Lay a seaweed sheet on top of a bamboo rolling mat or on the counter. (A mat will really help with the rolling process, and wrapping it tightly with plastic wrap will speed cleanup.) Place half of the rice on top of the seaweed sheet and spread it evenly all over, leaving 1 to 1½ inches uncovered at the top edge. Arrange half each of the jalapeño, chives, omelet, carrot, mint, and pea shoots in a row (they can mingle) across the center of the rice. Gently roll the mat away from you, keeping the filling in place with your thumbs. Using a little water, seal the top of the roll. Remove the roll from the mat and set aside. Repeat with the remaining ingredients to make a second roll. Brush the rolls with the sesame oil for that fresh kimbap shine.

4 Cut each roll crosswise into slices ½ to ¾ inch thick, arrange on a plate, and serve.

Pickled Jalapeño

1 To make the pickling liquid, in a small saucepan, combine the sugar, soy sauce, and vinegar and bring to a boil over medium-high heat, stirring to dissolve the sugar. Remove from the heat and let cool for 15 minutes.

2 Put the jalapeños into a small bowl and pour the pickling liquid over them. Cover and refrigerate for 4 hours before using. They will keep in an airtight container in the refrigerator for up to 1 week.

½ cup sugar

½ cup light soy sauce

¾ cup rice vinegar

6 medium jalapeños, stemmed and cut crosswise into ⅛-inch-thick slices, with seeds

Kimbap Rice

Put the rice into a small bowl. Add the oil and salt and mix well.

1 cup cooked rice (page 205), cooled to room temperature

2 teaspoons sesame oil

½ teaspoon kosher salt

Candied Anchovies

1 In a small, heavy saucepan, heat the neutral oil over medium-high heat to 250°F. Add the anchovies and fry, stirring constantly, until light golden and crisp, about 10 minutes. Make sure the exhaust fan in your range hood is working, as this will produce some serious anchovy vapor. All worth it in the end.

2 Remove from the heat and pour the contents of the pan into a fine-mesh (metal) sieve placed over a heatproof container (reserve the oil for another use or discard it). Return the anchovies to the hot pan, place over low heat, add the mirin, and deglaze the pan, stirring to dislodge all the browned bits from the pan bottom. Working quickly and stirring constantly, fold in the sugar and soy sauce and finish with the sesame oil. Season with salt to taste and remove from the heat.

1 cup neutral cooking oil

5 ounces dried baby anchovies (jiri myeolchi)

1 tablespoon mirin

2 tablespoons sugar

1 teaspoon soy sauce

½ teaspoon sesame oil

Kosher salt

Pineapple Kimchi

MAKES ABOUT 4 CUPS

1 In a blender, combine the pear, gochugaru, fish sauce, garlic, sugar, and ginger and blend until smooth to make the marinade.

2 In a large pickling jar or lidded container, combine the pineapple and as much of the marinade as you like and stir to coat. (Use the remaining marinade with other vegetables like daikon or napa cabbage.) Cover and refrigerate for 2 hours before using. The kimchi will keep in the refrigerator for up to 1 week, but honestly, it's not going to last that long.

½ cup chopped Asian pear

½ cup coarsely ground gochugaru

¼ cup fish sauce

2 garlic cloves

2 tablespoons sugar

2 teaspoons roughly chopped fresh ginger

1 large pineapple, peeled, cored, and cut into 1-inch cubes

KAWIBAP
카위밥

MAKES 2 ROLLS; SERVES 1

Open from only 2019 to 2021, Momofuku Kāwi was a short-lived though influential and slightly experimental restaurant from David Chang and chef Eunjo Park. Many regarded the restaurant as David Chang's first "true Korean" restaurant, and under the guidance of Park, it served up many classic dishes written with a Per Se and Momofuku Ko veteran's fine-point pen. Tteokbokki with Benton's ham and chile jam and tofu brûlée were two classics from Park's deep repertoire, but it was her kimbap, including this signature kawibap, that lives on.

This kimbap is built around candied baby anchovies, available at Korean grocers, which bring an incredible sweetness and crunch to the rice roll, which also includes pickled chile and egg.

OMELET
2 eggs

1 tablespoon extra-virgin olive oil

Two 6-inch roasted sheets nori seaweed (kim)

1 cup Kimbap Rice (see page 213)

½ cup drained Pickled Jalapeño (see page 213)

1 bunch chives

6 tablespoons Candied Anchovies (see page 213)

1 teaspoon sesame oil

Sea urchin roe and salmon roe, for serving (optional but highly recommended)

1. **Make the rolled omelet:** In a small bowl, whisk the eggs until blended. In a medium skillet, heat the olive oil over low heat. The pan should not be too hot or the delicate eggs will overcook. Pour the whisked eggs into the pan, swirl the pan to coat the bottom evenly, and cook until the eggs are set, about 2 minutes. Once they are set, holding an offset spatula in each hand, carefully roll the egg toward your body until you have a thick, rolled omelet log. Transfer to a plate and let sit for several minutes.

2. **Assemble the kimpap:** Lay a seaweed sheet on top of a bamboo mat or on the counter. (A mat will really help with the rolling process, and wrapping it tightly with plastic wrap will speed cleanup.) Place half the rice on top of the seaweed sheet and spread it evenly all over, leaving 1 to 1½ inches uncovered at the top edge. Arrange half each of the jalapeño, chives, and omelet and 3 tablespoons of the anchovies in a row (they can mingle) across the center of the rice.

3. Gently roll the mat away from you, keeping the filling in place with your thumbs. Using a little water, seal the top of the roll. Remove the roll from the mat and set aside. Repeat with the remaining ingredients to make a second roll. Brush the rolls with the sesame oil for that fresh kimbap shine.

4. Cut each roll crosswise into slices ½ to ¾ inch thick, arrange on a plate, and serve with sea urchin and salmon roe on the side (if using).

PINEAPPLE KIMCHI BOKKEUMBAP
PINEAPPLE KIMCHI FRIED RICE
파인애플 김치볶음밥

SERVES 4

Honestly, we've been flattered to see our method for pineapple kimchi, developed in 2014, replicated and evolved on menus and in recipes around the world, like Danny Bowien's great vegan version in *Mission Vegan*. But here we're taking it a step further and mashing it up with another fan-favorite recipe, our mildly insane kimchi bokkeumbap (we went a little heavy with the kimchi butter). This really cool version of kimchi fried rice is sweet, tangy, and full of the carby pleasure of a good fried rice.

Pineapple is commonly found in Southeast Asian fried rice, mainly Thai versions, and the kimchi variation used here (see page 213) serves as an amazing backbone for a dish that can be put together in under twenty minutes. Four cups drained canned pineapple chunks can be substituted for fresh.

SEASONING

2 tablespoons fish sauce

2 tablespoons sesame oil

2 tablespoons Pineapple Kimchi juice (see page 213)

1 tablespoon soy sauce

2 tablespoons gochugaru

2 tablespoons brown sugar

1 tablespoon gochujang

3 tablespoons neutral cooking oil

6 garlic cloves, minced

1-inch knob fresh ginger, minced

1 cup small-diced onion

1 red bell pepper, seeded and diced small

6 scallions, white and green parts, thinly sliced

4 cups day-old cooked short-grain rice, cold

2 cups drained Pineapple Kimchi, diced (see page 213)

4 eggs, beaten

1 **Make the seasoning:** In a small bowl, combine all the ingredients and mix well. Set aside.

2 In a wok or large sauté pan, heat the neutral oil over medium-high heat until it shimmers. Add the garlic, ginger, onion, red pepper, and half the scallions and cook, stirring often, until very aromatic, 1 to 2 minutes.

3 Add the rice and seasoning mixture, raise the heat to high, and cook, stirring constantly, until well mixed, about 1 minute. Add the kimchi and cook, stirring frequently, until well mixed and very hot, 4 to 5 minutes longer.

4 Push the rice to one side of the pan. Add the eggs to the empty side of the pan and cook, stirring gently occasionally, until scrambled and just set. Mix the eggs into the rice mixture, distributing them evenly.

5 Divide the rice among four bowls (or carved-out pineapple halves). Garnish with the remaining scallions and serve immediately.

RETHINKING HOT POT EXCELLENCE WITH HAN OAK'S PETER CHO

Eater has called Peter Cho and Sun Young Park "Portland's chillest culinary power couple," and they are two of the nicest folks you will meet in the food world. They're behind Han Oak (meaning a version of "home" in Korean), the city's now-legendary restaurant, casual backyard hangout space, karaoke den, and ambitious live-work kitchen. When it opened in 2016, it served high-end Korean barbecue, but Cho—a *Food & Wine* Best New Chef—reiterated the concept many times over the years.

For example, they've done Korean fried chicken seasoned with Shin Ramyun and family-style bossam (seasoned boiled pork). They've done late-night karaoke parties and wine dinners featuring some of Oregon's top winemakers paired with Korean cooking (including CHO Wines, the first Korean American wine company in America). Most recently, when we visited a couple of times in 2022, Cho was focused on perfecting a multicourse, fixed-price hot pot meal—an interpretation of the traditional Korean communal dish known as jeongol.

He calls it "a tableside experience centered around a pot of our bone broth supreme," which he describes as inspired by the Chinese superior stock method of long-simmering beef, pork, and chicken meat and bones along with aromatics. He adds dried shiitake and seaweed to his version. Cho serves his large-format hot pot with a tray of dry-aged meats (including a house-made corned beef chadol), dumplings, noodles, a lineup of ssamjangs (dipping sauces) and hot mustard, and a basket of ssam (lettuce wraps). He ends with a butter juk (rice porridge) that is topped with cheffy items like caviar, marinated raw salmon belly, and pickled Dungeness crab that tips to the fine-dining luxury that could be in the couple's future. But for now, it's hot pot cooked out of a garage, and that's working quite well.

Cho was born in Korea and grew up in Portland, Oregon, attending college at the University of Oregon down the road in Eugene. After nearly a decade in New York City working as a trusted April Bloomfield lieutenant at places like the Spotted Pig, he returned to Portland in 2016 to open the semi-hidden and critically acclaimed Han Oak. Today, he runs two restaurants in addition to Han Oak: a dinner and brunch spot in downtown Portland and a wood-fired Korean barbecue restaurant that was just getting off the ground when this book was sent to print.

When we visited on a miraculously sunny winter Sunday in January 2023, Cho was in the middle of taking over a lease and getting his kitchen in check. But squarely on his mind during our visit was serving us all bowls of juk, which he made while his staff and friends sipped glasses of pét-nat produced by a Korean couple in the Willamette Valley and gossiped about restaurant news—really, just being chill.

The future is bright for Korean food in Portland, and during our visits we were deeply impressed with how a small though highly vocal community of Korean Americans has changed the way a city thinks about Korean food—a city that less than a decade ago was hardly taking notice.

BOTTOM-OF-THE-POT BUTTER JUK
버터죽

SERVES 2 TO 4

Peter Cho, chef-owner of Han Oak in Portland, Oregon, is one of the country's most accomplished Korean chefs. His success can be traced to a cool, easygoing attitude and an inventive, highly personal style of service. This end-of-meal juk is for all of those folks who don't know what to do with the end of a pot of jjigae, tang (soup), or any other brothy, large-format jeongol (hot pot). The answer is pretty simple: make a rice porridge using cooked rice, an egg, and butter to emulsify, and season it simply with salt and pepper, lemon zest, and seaweed. And if you want to be all cheffy, you can garnish it with some of that caviar you might have lying around. Alternatively, you can make this from scratch for a light lunch or dinner.

While the restaurant uses a "bone broth supreme," we are calling for our basic Anchovy Stock here. But feel free to use any broth or flavorful stock thing you have on hand. This is a dead-simple way to clean up a bowl of soup or stew and create an entire second meal in the process.

Note: This dish was originally developed to be the final course of a hot pot meal; in that scenario, you would strain the flavorful broth from the hot pot at the end of a meal and use that liquid. Feel free to add more liquid to equal 4 cups, or just have a thicker dish if you have less broth.

4 cups Anchovy Stock (page 47) or other flavorful stock (see Note)

1 cup cooked white rice

1 egg

2 tablespoons unsalted butter, cubed

Two or three 6-inch squares roasted nori seaweed (kim), cut into ribbons

Grated zest of 1 lemon

Kosher salt and ground black pepper

Salmon roe, caviar, Dungeness crabmeat, and/or sliced raw scallops, for garnish (optional)

1 In a medium saucepan, heat 1 cup of the stock over medium heat. Add the rice and egg and stir together with the stock until fully incorporated but the egg is not scrambled.

2 Add the butter and stir as it slowly melts to emulsify.

3 Turn up the heat to high and slowly add the remaining stock, 1 cup at a time, while constantly stirring (risotto style) until most, if not all, of the stock is used. The result should be a porridge-like consistency with a slightly thickened texture from the egg and butter.

4 Season with the seaweed, lemon zest, and salt and pepper. Garnish with one or more of the luxurious toppers if you like and serve.

TACO BELL BIBIMBAP
타코벨 비빔밥

SERVES 4

"Spiritually, a Taco Bell Power Menu Bowl is bibimbap, if you think about it," says Dennis Lee, the genius Chicago-based food writer behind *Food is Stupid*, one of our favorite newsletters. This recipe is the object lesson of his argument: you order that aforementioned rice bowl topped with little mounds of ingredients (sound familiar?) and Korean-ify it. Here's Dennis:

If you're not in the mood to be weighed down by a bazinga Doritos Double Decker Burrito Supreme, a leaner and meaner Power Menu Bowl is a demure option. But if you're at Taco Bell, who wants that? That's why the Power Menu Bowl Bibimbap exists in my world. Obviously, Korean ingredients play perfectly well with Mexican ones (loosely, in this case, as I'm not sure avocado ranch dressing is an heirloom ingredient from Oaxaca). Combined with American fast food, the result is a true trinity of power that'll bring you to your goddamn knees, and it's barely any work to make at home.

One Power Menu Bowl from Taco Bell contains chicken or steak (I prefer the latter), seasoned rice, black beans, shredded cheese, shredded lettuce, tomatoes, guacamole, sour cream, and the aforementioned avocado ranch sauce. Combined with traditional bibimbap ingredients (gochujang, namul, a fried egg), you've got a merger of multiple worlds and a fast dinner. Trust me, you're not ready for this.

8 Taco Bell hot sauce packets of choice (my personal favorite is Diablo, which is the spiciest)

¼ cup gochujang

½ cup Taco Bell Avocado Ranch Sauce

1 tablespoon sesame oil

2 or 3 Taco Bell Power Menu Bowls with meat of your choice, harvested straight from the drive-through (ask for the ranch sauce on the side)

2 cups cooked white rice, hot

3 portions of three different banchan of your choice, such as sigeumchi namul (sautéed spinach), kongnamul (bean sprouts), gosari namul (fernbrake), raw shredded carrot, sautéed shiitake mushrooms, kimchi—anything and everything goes as long as it's Korean

4 eggs, fried sunny-side up

Sesame seeds, for garnish

1   In a small bowl, whisk together the contents of the sauce packets and the gochujang until well mixed. In a separate small bowl, stir together the ranch sauce and oil until well mixed.

2   Carefully extract the seasoned rice from each Power Menu Bowl, add to a medium bowl, add the plain cooked rice, and mixed well. Divide among four bowls.

3   Carefully top each bowl with the remaining contents of the Power Menu Bowls (meat, beans, sour cream), trying to keep each component as separate as possible (this will be messy; do your best). Finish topping each bowl with the three banchan in separate mounds.

4   Place a fried egg on top of each bowl, then drizzle with the gochujang–Taco Bell sauce packet sauce and the ranch sauce–sesame oil mixture.

5   Sprinkle sesame seeds on top and serve immediately.

LET'S

TALK

ABOUT

FUSION

The term *fusion cuisine* has been used flatly to describe the union of two or more foods from seemingly different sources. Some of these foods originate within the same culture, with the cronut, a merging of two Eurocentric pastries (croissant and doughnut), being a classic example. Other times, the blending mashes up very different cultures, such as a masala cheesesteak prepared at a Chicago barbecue restaurant or the pepperoni pizza dumpling served at Smorgasburg in Los Angeles. This is hybrid cooking whether the application of the term is correct or not.

For us, fusion is not mayhem, and it's certainly not "the new F-word," as some have described it. It's the celebration of a culinary marriage: big ideas presented on small plates. And in Korean cooking specifically, though also universally, fusion has often started with creative instinct ("Hey, wouldn't kimchi make a bomb arancini filling?") and ended with sharp execution. In this chapter, we celebrate the collision of ideas that our friend the chef Dale Talde once called "natural fusion." For Ann Arbor chef Ji Hye Kim, a logical fit was substituting kkaennip (the Korean perilla that is like a sturdier type of shiso) for basil in a delicious pesto. For Madison, Wisconsin, chef Tory Miller, it meant lacing a traditional pimento cheese with kimchi for a brand-new spread—that also makes a killer grilled cheese. For Washington, DC, chef Angel Barreto, it was channeling the street-fair staple mozzarella arepa (MozzAprepa) into a summer corn pajeon. In Seoul it means kimbap topped with truffle mayo.

Fusion is nothing new in Korea—and we counter that idea with many examples in the Modern Korea section. Did you check out Deuki's definitively Korean cheesy corn dog on a stick (page 51) or cook some tteokbokki dotted with cream (page 35)? Fusion is loud and proud in Korean cooking, and we hope you enjoy these recipes that push the definition to the limit.

WASHINGTON, DC, CHEF ANGEL BARRETO IS STARTING MANY CONVERSATIONS

At Anju, his nearly always bursting at the seams Washington, DC, restaurant, Angel Barreto once served soondae, the traditional Korean blood sausage, in the "Egg McMuffin way," which coalesced as a breakfast sandwich built with soondae patties (flavored with garlic, ginger, black pepper, gochugaru, paprika, thyme, and sea salt) and a Cheddar biscuit spiced with Korean chile. It was a brunch hit with the hungry Dupont Circle crowd and remained a menu fixture for months— creatively bridging the gap between traditional halmoni (grandmother) cooking and Western hangover traditions for the laced-up DC crew that Barreto describes as relative Korean food novices. "Ninety-five percent of our clientele has not had Korean food," he says with his trademark smile, though he admits that diplomats, congressional leaders, and possibly two sitting Supreme Court justices are fans of the restaurant too. It is clear, which Barreto humbly acknowledges when the topic comes up, that he's playing a big role in changing the way Americans view Korean food. He's a James Beard Foundation award finalist and one of *Food & Wine*'s prestigious (and way legit) Best New Chefs.

But to some, Barreto is an unlikely ambassador for Korean food. His parents are Black and Puerto Rican, and while serving in the military, they moved the family every few years before his father settled in an intelligence role at the White House, where he served under Bill Clinton and George W. Bush and retired during the Obama administration. Barreto's parents met in Korea, and the food traditions they encountered there stuck; from an early age, Barreto was eating mandu and his mom's kimbap, boiling jjigaes, and loving every second of it. He initially wanted to work in politics and planned to study international relations at George Mason University. But after a disenchanting internship experience and the prospects of culinary school shaking him from a Beltway-oriented cruise control, he took the leap and has not looked back.

Anju is the term for Korean "drinking food," and the namesake restaurant that Barreto and his partner, Danny Lee (see page 162), have built certainly knows how to have a good time. (The restaurant has its own karaoke machine,

though it's just for staff.) But focusing on conviviality doesn't mean the culinary ambition has been taken down even an inch. One of the all-time favorite Korean dishes we encountered while traveling around the United States is Barreto's whole fish (saengseon gui), in which a branzino is lightly battered and fried and then served with fork-tender braised Korean radish and yangnyeom sauce (the gochujang-based lacquer found at Korean fried chicken restaurants). Barreto makes his sauce with garlic, ginger, soy sauce, perilla and sesame seeds, rice vinegar, and sugar, and it dresses the fish in the lightest and brightest way. The accompanying banchan is an inspired selection of Brussels sprout kimchi, candied lotus root, and soy sauce–brined chayote. In the summer months, the restaurant has served bingsu (shaved ice) inspired by the culinary teams' favorite childhood desserts (apple crumble and Fun Dip included).

Sometimes Barreto does a web search for "anju restaurant" to check out other restaurants around the world that are inspired by Korean drinking food. He's found spots in Singapore and Canada, and he thinks it's awesome that Korean food is spreading around the globe. "We want to be propagators and educators of somebody else's cuisine. This cooking we are doing is the start of a conversation, and there is so much more." How do you express a cuisine that has expanded so much in the past fifty years, from the time of the Miracle on the Han River (Korea's period of rapid economic growth following the Korean War) until now? Barreto sits on the question for a beat. "It's amazing, and I don't know." After spending some time at Anju, it's pretty clear he's on his way to finding out.

CORN JEON WITH SEASONED ONION SALAD

옥수수전과 양파샐러드

MAKES 4 HEARTY PANCAKES

Right around the time we were hanging out with Angel Barreto at his restaurant Anju in Washington, DC, TikTok blew up with the cutest kid expressing his love of corn. (If you haven't seen it, Google "Corn Kid Recess Therapy" and be prepared to say "It's corn!" over and over.) Well, Barreto (like us) is down with corn, too, and he has a really delicious play on the traditional Korean pajeon using fresh corn and mozzarella cheese. The crispy, gooey, corny pancake is now one of our summertime staples, but this dish hardly has to be seasonal fare. Frozen corn works just as well as fresh. A standard-issue (H Mart–procured) jeon mix works great here. And pile each pancake with a seasoned onion salad. While "It's onion" doesn't roll off the tongue quite as well, it's the perfect addition to this savory pancake.

ONION SALAD

¼ white onion, thinly sliced (Barreto uses a mandoline)

1 tablespoon sesame oil

Kosher salt and ground black pepper

PANCAKES

1¼ cups jeon mix

¾ cup water

¾ cup fresh or frozen corn kernels

¼ cup thinly sliced scallions, white and green parts

2 teaspoons peeled, grated fresh ginger

1 teaspoon minced garlic

1 tablespoon sesame oil

2 teaspoons kosher salt

1 teaspoon ground black pepper

1½ cups shredded mozzarella cheese

Neutral cooking oil, for cooking

Fresh mint leaves, for garnish

1. **Make the onion salad:** In a small bowl, drizzle the onion with the sesame oil, season with salt and pepper, and mix well. Set aside.

2. **Make the pancakes:** In a medium bowl, combine the jeon mix, water, corn, scallions, ginger, garlic, sesame oil, salt, pepper, and ½ cup of the cheese and stir together until well mixed.

3. In a medium skillet, heat ¼ cup neutral oil over medium heat until it shimmers. Ladle about ½ cup of the batter into the middle of the pan and, using the back of the ladle, smooth the batter until evenly thick and about 7 inches in diameter. Cook until golden, about 2 minutes. Flip and cook on the other side until golden, about 2 minutes. Lift the pancake, scatter ¼ cup of the cheese under it, and then continue to cook the pancake until the cheese has browned and is crunchy all over, about 2 minutes longer. Transfer to a plate and keep warm. Repeat with the remaining batter and cheese to make three more pancakes.

4. Top the pancakes with the onion salad, then garnish with mint and serve immediately.

SHAVED BRUSSELS SPROUT, KIMCHI, AND WATERMELON SALAD WITH YUJA DRESSING

방울양배추김치

SERVES 4

Brussels sprouts are typically associated with fall and winter roasting, but there's a modern tradition of chefs thinly shaving the tiny cabbages and serving them as the base of a hearty salad. Angel Barreto of Anju in Washington, DC, is also a fan of shaved Brussels sprouts, and he has served a version of this summer-meets-autumn salad at his restaurant. The base can be rotated – sub in fresh corn, leafy greens, or mint – but the constant remains this incredible dressing made with yuja citron tea – a concentrated yuzu syrup found in many grocery stores. The dressing recipe yields more than you need for this salad, but it keeps well and can be used for future salad making or marinades.

½ pound Brussels sprouts

2 cups peeled, cubed watermelon

1 cup cherry tomatoes, halved

1 cup peeled, shredded carrots

1 cup shredded fresh green cabbage

½ cup drained, chopped cabbage kimchi

¼ cup toasted pine nuts

½ cup Yuja Salad Dressing, or as needed (recipe follows)

1   Trim the Brussels sprouts. Then, using a mandoline or a sharp knife, thinly shave them lengthwise. You should have about 4 cups. Transfer them to a large bowl. Add the watermelon, tomatoes, carrots, fresh cabbage, cabbage kimchi, and pine nuts.

2   Drizzle the dressing over the salad and toss gently to coat evenly. Taste and adjust with more dressing if desired, then serve.

Yuja Salad Dressing

유자 샐러드 드레싱

MAKES 3 CUPS

1   In a blender, combine all the ingredients and pulse until well mixed, 15 to 20 seconds. Make sure the yuja cha is fully incorporated and free of lumps.

2   Use immediately, or transfer to an airtight container and store in the refrigerator for up to 2 weeks.

1 cup canola oil

1 cup mirin

½ cup yuja cha (honey citron tea)

½ cup rice vinegar

1 tablespoon sugar

Grated zest and juice of 1 lemon

1 tablespoon ground black pepper

KIMCHI-BRAISED SHORT RIB PAPPARDELLE

갈비 김치찜 파파르델레

SERVES 4 TO 6

Eric Kim is our dude! He's a force in not just Korean home cooking but *all* home cooking, working as a staff writer at New York Times Cooking, where his recipes often seamlessly incorporate Korean flavors and ideas into a global repertoire of dishes. A copy of his highly personal and enjoyable book, *Korean American,* is splattered with soy sauce and sits on the counter in Matt's home kitchen. When we asked Kim to contribute a recipe for the book, he jumped right in with this play on the classic braised and warming kimchi jjim. "This is a great example of kimchi in its last state: cooked down and absolutely melting," he says of this meaty braised kimchi pasta that we've already made many times.

1½ pounds English-cut, bone-in beef short ribs

Kosher salt and ground black pepper

Extra-virgin olive oil, for cooking

2 cups water

2 cups drained napa cabbage kimchi, roughly chopped

½ large yellow onion, thinly sliced

4 large garlic cloves

3 tablespoons gochugaru

2 tablespoons soy sauce

1 tablespoon sugar

1 tablespoon sesame oil

1 pound dried pappardelle or other wide pasta noodle

Finely chopped fresh flat-leaf parsley, for seasoning

Wedge of Parmesan cheese, for serving

1   Preheat the oven to 325°F.

2   Season the short ribs generously with salt and pepper. Heat a Dutch oven or other large, heavy pot over medium-high heat. Add enough olive oil to coat the bottom and heat until it shimmers. Then add the short ribs and sear, turning once, until browned on both sides, about 8 minutes total. Using tongs, transfer the short ribs to a plate.

3   With the pot still over medium-high heat, add the water, kimchi, onion, garlic, gochugaru, soy sauce, sugar, and sesame oil, stir together well, and bring to a simmer. Nestle the ribs, bone side up, in the pot. They should be mostly, if not completely, covered by the liquid.

4   Cover the pot, transfer to the oven, and bake until the short ribs are meltingly tender (the meat should fall off the bone when poked with a fork or spoon), the liquid has reduced by about half, and the kimchi and onions have melted into jammy submission, 2½ to 3 hours.

5   Remove the pot from the oven and use a spoon or ladle to skim the fat from the surface. Carefully remove the short ribs and any bones that may have slipped free of the meat from the pot. Discard the bones and shred the meat with two forks. Return the meat to the pot.

6   Meanwhile, bring a large pot of water to a boil over high heat. Season it generously with salt, add the pappardelle, and cook, stirring occasionally, until about 2 minutes shy of al dente, according to the package instructions. (The pasta will finish cooking in the sauce.) Using tongs, transfer the pasta from its cooking pot directly to the pot holding the meat and sauce.

7   Set the pot over medium heat. Using tongs, toss the sauce with the pasta until the sauce reduces, becomes thicker and richer, and thinly coats the pasta, about 2 minutes. Taste and adjust the seasoning with salt and pepper if needed.

8   To serve, add as much parsley to the pasta as you like and toss to mix well. Serve the Parmesan with a grater for guests to help themselves.

KKAENNIP PESTO
깻잎 페스토

MAKES ABOUT ¾ CUP

Ji Hye Kim is a *Food & Wine* Best New Chef and has been nominated for multiple James Beard Foundation awards for her work at the progressive Korean restaurant Miss Kim in Ann Arbor, Michigan. She's also a scholar of the Korean cooking game and wants to write a book about Joseon dynasty cuisine. But this recipe takes its inspiration not just from Korea but also from Italy and the Genoese pesto Hye adores making at the height of summer when basil grows like a weed. Here, she trades out basil for the floral herb perilla (known as kkaennip in Korean and a relative of the Japanese shiso), and it's such a winning idea.

Marinated kkaennip is often served as a refreshing banchan and is occasionally panfried into fritters. A pesto made from kkaennip lands pretty close to the original, though the fish sauce shapes the final product into something distinct, deep, and craveable. Ji Hye's first instinct is to serve this with toasted rice cakes — "the ones used for tteokbokki" — but it will go well with pasta or rice noodles too.

As you make this recipe, simply follow the ratio but know that plenty of substitutes would work. Most nuts will do, but toasted sesame seeds will also work just great. Fish sauce is not required, though you might want to think before you skip it, as it adds great depth. For vegetarians, you can use the more traditional grated Parmesan in its place. If you can't find perilla, shiso will give you a similar flavor. Finally, feel free to add more lemon juice or zest for added zip.

2 cups hand-torn, lightly packed perilla leaves (about 20 leaves)

¼ cup toasted pine nuts or walnuts

2 teaspoons fish sauce

2 teaspoons freshly squeezed lemon juice

4 garlic cloves

¾ cup extra-virgin olive oil

1 In a blender, combine the perilla leaves, pine nuts, fish sauce, lemon juice, and garlic and pulse several times until chopped. With the blender running, slowly add the oil, a few tablespoons at a time, and blend until the pesto is smooth.

2 Use immediately, or transfer to an airtight container and store in the refrigerator for up to 1 week.

Serving Suggestions

Toss with sautéed rice cakes and garnish generously with shredded roasted nori seaweed (kim) and toasted pine nuts or sesame seeds.

Toss with somyeon noodles and garnish as for rice cakes.

Toss with rice noodles and garnish as for rice cakes.

Toss with shell pasta, cherry tomatoes, and pulled cooked chicken for a pasta salad.

Spread on bread for avocado toast.

DOUBLE JANG MEAT MARINADE
캠핑 고기 양념

MAKES 2 CUPS

Daniel Holzman, Matt's good friend and writing partner, is a chef and the founder of The Meatball Shop and Danny Boy's Famous Original. While working on a column for *Saveur* and their book *Food IQ,* they've eaten sticky pork ribs at Ham Ji Park and seolleongtang at Master Ha in Los Angeles, grilled over hot coals in Queens, and sampled wildly fermented banchan in Copenhagen.

Inspired by his love of doenjang and gochujang, Holzman created this meat marinade, and it's been in heavy rotation for him for years. Jang, vinegar, sesame oil, and the defining sweetness of honey make for a marinade that is reminiscent of Kansas City barbecue sauce but with the heat and intensity you can only get from fermentation.

It's great both as a marinade and a table sauce (once it's thinned out with a little water). Use it with beef, pork, or chicken. The best bet is to marinate the meat overnight and fire it over a backyard grill or broil it in the oven. Holzman is most excited when he's using it with tri-tip, chicken legs, and pork chops. Just be aware that the combination of honey and jangs can burn quickly, causing a bitter flavor, so watch for those char spots.

¾ cup doenjang
¾ cup gochujang
¼ cup rice vinegar
¼ cup honey
1 tablespoon sesame oil
2 to 5 pounds meat or poultry of your choice

1   In a large bowl, whisk together the doenjang, gochujang, vinegar, honey, and oil, mixing well. The perfume of the jangs will hit you hard (in the best way).

2   Using your hands, place the meat in the marinade and massage it in. This can include chicken legs, wings, and thighs; rib eye; pork loin or chops; baby back ribs; or any meat that is fit for the grill. Cover and refrigerate overnight for the best result.

3   Remove the meat from the marinade, shaking off any excess, and let sit at room temperature for 30 minutes or so before cooking.

4   **To grill:** Prepare a charcoal or gas grill for direct cooking over medium-high heat. To check if it's ready, place your hand 6 inches above the grate; you should be able to withstand the heat for only 5 seconds before pulling away. Working in batches that fit comfortably in a single layer on the grate, grill the meat or poultry to the desired temperature, then serve.

5   **To broil:** Position a rack in the upper third of the oven and preheat the broiler. Place the meat or poultry in a single layer on a broiler pan, slide onto the top rack, and broil, turning frequently so as not to burn, to the desired temperature, then serve.

THE BIRTH OF THE KIM JONG GRILLIN KIMCHI AND PICKLED MANGO DOG

Han Ly Hwang is the owner of the popular roving restaurant and food cart Kim Jong Grillin. Hwang grew up in Northern Virginia and found his way to Portland, Oregon, where he became a journeyman line cook and "cooked wherever I was needed for whoever paid the best tips" before founding his food truck nearly a decade ago.

The years of work have paid off, and he's now earned a reputation for his creativity (his kalbi is made with Sunkist strawberry soda) and hospitality within the close-knit Portland food scene. Hwang's rise is emblematic of Korean food's transferred energy in America, from the OG for-us-by-us barbecue grills and soup sellers of the past to the present, where a freestanding Korean food truck can be named the best food truck in America's preeminent food-truck town. His most popular menu item, hands down, is a spicy kimchi hot dog topped with pickled mango. We fell hard for it during one of our many trips to the SE Division Street truck, and we wanted to find out about its genesis, which Hwang was happy to share:

When I opened Kim Jong Grillin, I knew I had to put a hot dog on the menu. It got so complicated in my brain. At one point, I tried to make a jajangmyeon [noodles with black bean sauce] hot dog, and then a failed jjamppong [spicy seafood noodle soup] hot dog.

And then I just gave up. Fuck a hot dog! What's so great about having a hot dog on the menu anyway? Well, because, America. That's why. I needed a bridge for white America to try the other stuff on my menu. A hot dog is unassuming and low-risk for Portlanders!

Fast-forward a year, and I took a trip to Hawaii. I stopped at a stand on the side of the road to buy fruit and a $40 coconut from a vendor, 'cause I'm an asshole with a rental car on an island. And then there it was . . . pickled mango. It was so cold and sour and sweet and refreshing. This was what I was missing.

When I put together the hot dog, I found the right bread from a Vietnamese bakery that has been making baguettes in Portland for twenty-plus years. This is one of those spots you don't go to without an Asian

friend as a cosigner. I worked out a deal and was able to wholesale the bread from her. It took me like two months, but here we are, nine years later, and I'm still able to pick up bread from her.

Mexican mayonesa has that hit of lime juice that completes the finish of our sour kimchi, and the banchan—sprouts with sesame oil and shredded daikon—complete each other texturally when they're on bread.

When I assembled the first KJG hot dog, it was amazing. I might have cried, not because it tasted amazing but because I finally figured out this weird puzzle in my head. We all have a dish that evokes our version of what "good" tastes like. This one happens to be mine.

KIM JONG GRILLIN PICKLED MANGO AND KIMCHI HOT DOG

김치 핫도그

MAKES 2 HOT DOGS

The mangoes are one of the key components of this simple yet complex hot dog. Start with a toasted banh mi baguette and add kimchi mayonnaise, which is simply a mix of Mexican mayonesa and extra-sour kimchi. Seasoned bean sprouts and daikon banchan are added, and the dish is finished with the pickled mango. "We sell out of these daily, and it has become a cult favorite around here," says Kim Jong Grillin owner Han Ly Hwang.

2 hot dogs (foot longs work best)

Two 10- to 12-inch soft baguettes or other crusty sandwich buns

½ cup Kimchi Mayo (recipe follows)

½ cup bean sprout banchan

½ cup shredded daikon banchan

½ cup extra-sour cabbage kimchi

½ cup Pickled Mango (recipe follows)

1 Prepare a charcoal or gas grill for direct cooking over medium-high heat. To check if it's ready, place your hand 6 inches above the grate; you should be able to withstand the heat for only 5 seconds before pulling away. Or preheat a cast-iron grill pan on the stove top over medium-high heat. Grill the hot dogs, turning as needed, until the casing starts to break. Set aside.

2 Toast the cut sides of the baguettes on the grill or cast-iron pan until slightly charred but still soft, 30 seconds to 1 minute.

3 To assemble each hot dog, coat the cut side of the baguette with half of the mayo. Make a bed on the bottom half with half of the bean sprouts, place a hot dog on top, and then top with half each of the daikon, cabbage kimchi, and finally the mango. Serve immediately.

Kimchi Mayo
김치 마요

1   In a food processor or blender, combine the mayonesa and kimchi and process until smooth.

2   Use immediately, or transfer to an airtight container and store in the refrigerator for up to 2 weeks. Use on sandwiches or whatever bready thing needs a little boost.

1 cup mayonesa (Mexican mayonnaise)

½ cup drained extra-sour cabbage kimchi, very finely chopped

Pickled Mango
망고장아찌

MAKES ABOUT 1 CUP

1   Peel the mango, cut the flesh away from the pit, and julienne the flesh. Transfer to a small bowl.

2   Add the sugar and salt to the mango, toss together, and let sit for 10 to 15 minutes. The salt and sugar will leach the juice from the mango, which will form a syrup. There will be some undissolved salt and sugar left at the bottom of the bowl.

3   Add the vinegar in small amounts until the mango is barely covered with the juice and vinegar and then mix by hand.

4   At this point, the mango will have softened a bit but still be firm and is ready to eat. It will keep in an airtight container in the refrigerator for up to a week.

1 large hard, green (unripe) mango

¼ cup sugar

2 tablespoons kosher salt

About ½ cup distilled white vinegar or rice vinegar

DWAEJI BULGOGI ON A ROLL
SPICY PORK BULGOGI ON A ROLL
돼지불고기롤

MAKES 4 TO 6 SANDWICHES

Over the decade plus that Eric and Miriam Park have run various restaurants out of a space at 2852 Sunset Boulevard in Silver Lake, Los Angeles, the theme has remained consistent, even though the dishes have traveled the world — from Hawaiian poke and ají chicken burritos to the NYC bodega classic chopped cheese. The Eastside of LA can be a fickle dining neighborhood, but the Parks have remained a constant presence. While researching this book in early 2023, we caught the duo in one of their more ambitious and Korean-leaning phases, reflecting their shared heritage.

Although the Parks' take on the chopped cheese was stealing headlines and getting folks like actor Elijah Wood to become dedicated followers (he rolled up while we were visiting), we were most impressed with this creative pork bulgogi sandwich. Eric is one of LA's top sandwich chefs, and this one was created early in the COVID-19 pandemic. "When everyone was quarantining, our shop pivoted to making marinated meats that people could cook at home," Miriam explains. The pivot to selling pre-seasoned meat led to one of the restaurant's most popular items: an addictively sweet and savory pile of charred pork shoulder and belly tucked into a ciabatta roll that's coated with great mayonnaise and stacked with thick slices of raw onion. "A perfect sandwich, if you ask me," says Eric.

MARINADE

3-inch knob fresh ginger, peeled and roughly chopped

12 garlic cloves

1 large jalapeño, roughly chopped

3 scallions, white and green parts, roughly chopped

3 tablespoons mirin

3 tablespoons sesame oil

2 tablespoons soy sauce

4 teaspoons fish sauce

1 tablespoon gochugaru

½ cup gochujang

¼ cup firmly packed dark brown sugar

2 teaspoons kosher salt

1 pound boneless pork shoulder, thickly sliced

1 pound skinless pork belly, thickly sliced

1 to 2 tablespoons neutral cooking oil

4 to 6 hearty rolls (such as ciabatta), split

Good mayonnaise, for spreading (such as Duke's)

Thick white onion slices, for topping

1 **Make the marinade:** In a blender, combine the ginger, garlic, jalapeño, scallions, mirin, sesame oil, soy sauce, fish sauce, and gochugaru and puree until smooth.

2 Pour the pureed mixture into a large bowl, add the gochujang, sugar, and salt, and whisk together, mixing well. Transfer the marinade to a separate small container.

3 Add the pork shoulder and pork belly to the same bowl. Pour in half of the marinade and begin mixing the pork into it. Add more marinade as necessary to coat the pork generously. You'll have more marinade than you need. Transfer the remainder to an airtight container and save for another use. It will keep in the refrigerator for up to 2 weeks. Marinate the pork at room temperature for 30 minutes to 1 hour.

4 When you are ready to cook, set a cast-iron skillet over high heat and get it good and hot. Pour in enough neutral oil to coat the bottom of the pan and heat until it shimmers. Then begin cooking the marinated pork in batches, letting the excess marinade drip off the slices before adding them to the pan and being careful not to crowd them. Sear the pork, turning as needed, until nicely browned on both sides and with some char on the edges. As each batch is ready, transfer to a large plate and keep warm.

5 Toast the cut sides of the rolls. Spread the cut sides with mayo and layer the pork on the bottom halves. Top with the onion, cover with the top halves, and enjoy.

KIMCHEESE
김치이즈

SERVES 4 TO 6

Tory Miller is the chef to know in Madison, Wisconsin – one of America's great food cities and Matt's beloved college town. He's a multiple James Beard Foundation award winner and articulates his connection to Korean culture in an honest and open way. As a Korean adoptee, he's negotiated his blended background through food, and this amazing recipe blends pure Americana (pimento cheese) with kimchi with incredible results. Use this as a dip with crackers or crudités or as a burger topping or grilled cheese filling. Miller has added it to bao, put it in ramen, and used it as a base for a pretty incredible mac and cheese. It will keep in the fridge for a week (if it sticks around that long).

Note: Emojis have been left in for critical emphasis!

1 red bell pepper

8 ounces cream cheese, at room temperature

8 ounces aged Wisconsin Cheddar cheese, shredded (you can use other cheese but it will be garbage 😛)

12 ounces drained, finely chopped cabbage kimchi

¼ cup Kewpie or Duke's brand mayonnaise or whatever kind isn't Hellmann's or Best Foods 😇

1 tablespoon hot sauce (such as Frank's RedHot or Louisiana)

1½ teaspoons Worcestershire sauce

1 tablespoon gochugaru

1   Preheat the oven to 400°F. Line a small sheet pan with aluminum foil and place the pepper on it. Roast the pepper, turning it occasionally as needed to color evenly, until the skin is blistered and charred. Ideally it will be pretty black all over after about 20 minutes. When it is sufficiently black but not ash, place it in a bowl and cover the bowl with plastic wrap. Alternatively, scorch the pepper by carefully running it over the flame of a stove-top burner until it is blistered and charred all over, then transfer to a bowl and cover with plastic wrap. Let the pepper sit for at least 10 minutes or until cool enough to handle, then peel off the blackened skin and remove and discard the stem and seeds. Cut the pepper into small dice and transfer to a medium bowl.

2   Add the cream cheese to the bowl and, using a rubber spatula, mix well with the pepper. This helps loosen the cream cheese and get it ready to accept the rest of the ingredients.

3   Add the Cheddar, kimchi, mayonnaise, hot sauce, Worcestershire sauce, and gochugaru and mix until all the ingredients are fully incorporated.

4   Serve immediately, or transfer to an airtight container and store in the refrigerator for up to 1 week.

BINDAETTEOK, BACON, AND EGGS
빈대떡

MAKES 8 TO 10 PANCAKES

Jeon, Korean pancakes, are awesome, but if you've never had bindaetteok, we are excited to get to introduce them to you. Made with mung beans instead of wheat flour, a well-made bindaetteok is incredible. The crackly texture and earthy batter remind us of potato latkes. This is why it was so cool to see it served alongside bacon and eggs in Portland, Oregon, at Sue Gee Kehn's Cameo Café in the city's Northeast neighborhood.

Kehn opened the Portland location in 1992 (there's also one across the Columbia River in Vancouver, Washington), where she serves a killer bibimbap alongside a patty melt and a Monte Cristo. The restaurant's menu is mostly American-style brunch items (with an incredible homemade raspberry syrup for the short stacks). Kehn started adding Korean dishes as a simple tribute to her heritage, and many of the dishes stuck. During our visits, it was the crispy, savory pancake that drew us, and we've found this is the perfect breakfast if you want to use up leftover bulgogi — serve the beef alongside to make it steak and eggs. You can most certainly use a store-bought bindaetteok mix for this pancake, and there are some good ones available. But if you can find split mung beans (also sold as moong dal in South Asian markets) and make your own batter, the result will be great too. Serve this bacon, eggs, and bindaetteok spread with a side of kimchi, rice, and Yuja Chojang (page 133) and say good night before you say good afternoon.

2 cups dried split mung beans

1 cup drained cabbage kimchi, chopped

1 tablespoon sesame oil, plus more for drizzling

1 tablespoon soy sauce

1 teaspoon doenjang

¼ teaspoon kosher salt

½ cup water

Neutral cooking oil, for cooking

4 eggs

6 to 10 slices bacon or sausage links

1   Rinse the mung beans well, then transfer to a medium bowl, add water to cover, and let soak for 2 to 3 hours. Drain.

2   In a large bowl, combine the kimchi, sesame oil, soy sauce, doenjang, and salt and mix well. Set aside.

3   In a food processor, combine the mung beans and water and process until you have a mealy, sand-like consistency. Add the mung bean mixture to the kimchi mixture and mix well to form a batter.

4   To make the pancakes, place a medium skillet over medium-high heat and heat 3 tablespoons (or more) neutral oil until it shimmers. Ladle two silver-dollar-size pancakes into the pan, spacing them well apart, and cook, turning once and adding more oil to the pan for additional crispiness, until golden on both sides, 2 to 3 minutes on each side. Transfer to a plate and keep warm. Repeat with the remaining batter, adding more oil to the pan as needed.

5   While the pancakes are cooking, cook the bacon and eggs in your most relaxed way. Scrambled works and may be easiest if you're also on pancake duty, but sunny-side up is great.

6   When everything is ready, drizzle a little sesame oil on the pancakes, and serve immediately.

DAKDORI OYAKODON
닭도리 오야꼬동

SERVES 2

Chef and budding TV personality Daniel Harthausen is an exciting new voice in food, having won the first season of HBO's *The Big Brunch* and running the roving pop-up Young Mother in Richmond, Virginia. Harthausen was raised by a Japanese-Korean mother and a half-Korean father and "had a baseline of what really good Korean food tasted like without really knowing it at the time," he says.

This recipe merges Korean dakdori tang (spicy chicken stew) and the beloved Japanese donburi oyakodon (chicken and eggs over rice). It's spicy, comforting, and a great dinner party main course.

1 small russet potato

4 boneless, skinless chicken thighs

Kosher salt and ground black pepper

1 medium white or yellow onion, halved

3 garlic cloves

½-inch knob fresh ginger, peeled

½ cup sake

½ cup mirin

2 tablespoons gochujang

1 tablespoon oyster sauce

1 tablespoon honey

1 teaspoon gochugaru

1 teaspoon curry powder (preferably S&B brand)

Neutral cooking oil, for cooking

2 scallions, white and green parts, cut into 1-inch lengths with white and green kept separate

1 cup Anchovy Stock (page 47) or dashi (instant is fine)

1 bay leaf

2 eggs

2 to 3 cups cooked white rice

1   Have ready a small bowl of cold water. Peel the potato, then coarsely grate it directly into the bowl of water. Cut the chicken thighs into 1-inch-thick strips, then cut the strips in half crosswise, leaving pieces about 1 inch long. Season with salt and pepper and set aside.

2   In a food processor, combine half of the onion, the garlic, ginger, sake, and mirin and process, stopping as needed to push down any large chunks until a paste forms, about 1 minute. Add the gochujang, oyster sauce, honey, gochugaru, and curry powder and process until well mixed. Scrape the mixture into a small bowl and set aside.

3   Drain the potato and squeeze it to get rid of any excess liquid. Slice the remaining onion half.

4   In a large skillet, heat 1 tablespoon oil over medium heat until it shimmers. Add the chicken and sear for 2 minutes. Add the potato, sliced onion, scallion whites, and the gochujang mixture and stir well. Reduce the heat to medium-low and cook, stirring constantly and scraping the bottom of the pan to prevent scorching, for 1 minute.

5   Pour in the stock, stir to combine, raise the heat to high, and bring to a boil. Turn down the heat to low, add the bay leaf, and season with salt. Cover and simmer gently about 15 minutes.

6   While the chicken cooks, crack the eggs into a small bowl and add a pinch of salt. Don't fully whisk them. Instead, break the yolks gently and lift the whites to loosen them a bit. There should still be a slight separation between the whites and yolks.

7   After 15 minutes, uncover the skillet, raise the heat to medium, and add the reserved scallion greens. Once the pan is bubbling, add two-thirds of the egg mixture, dispersing it as evenly around the pan as possible. Let cook for 1 minute, then add the remaining egg mixture, again dispersing it evenly, and let cook for an additional 30 seconds. Turn off the heat and let sit for about 2 minutes.

8   Divide the rice between two big bowls, then divide the chicken mixture between the bowls, pouring it on top.

While dessert is never the focus of a Korean meal, the Korean dining landscape is peppered with cafés and convenience stores where snacking from plastic bags and microwavable bowls is a near art form. In the United States, where dessert is, of course, a big deal, Korean American restaurants have started to serve more and more plated desserts to close out the meal. The recipes in this chapter are a culmination of these trends, with kimchi salt–dusted popcorn, gochugaru-spiced caramel corn, a play on the dalgona candy trend, and a cake inspired by convenience-store banana milks (banana mat uyu). Closing out the chapter are a number of drinks, mostly nonalcoholic, that are all easy to make at home.

ARANG
KOREAN NACHOS
아랑나쵸

SERVES 4 TO 6

The mother-daughter team that ran longtime Thirty-Second Street pojangmacha Arang operated with a simple mantra. "We'll make tteokbokki dreams come true," read the slogan printed on the menu and website of the now long-shuttered New York City institution. And true to its claim, their version of the classic Korean rice cake dish haunts many 2:00 a.m. reveries.

Sue Song and her daughter, Sunny Lim, opened the original Arang on Thirty-Second Street in 2006. It was at that second-floor restaurant – which for years was popular with the post-noraebang crowd and played a soundtrack heavy on the Chromeo and "Freedom! '90" – that we were first introduced to Song's version of tteokbokki, which, in truth, is closer to Korean nachos. Same spongy tteok, same crimson gochujang-based sauce, then add a layer of stir-fried pork belly, white onion, Korean chiles, chopped kimchi, and nearly a *pound* of cheese (a blend of Cheddar and mozzarella). It's an incredible bite: the pork, the squishy rice cake, the kimchi, and the stringy cheese. We miss Arang and its amazing rice cakes, and we wanted to pay some respect with our take.

1   **Make the spicy pork:** In a blender, combine the onion, garlic, ginger, soy sauce, and water and blend until smooth. Transfer to a medium bowl, add the gochujang, gochugaru, honey powder, and mirin and mix well. Add the pork belly and stir to coat evenly. Cover and refrigerate for at least 2 hours or up to overnight.

2   Remove the pork from the refrigerator and preferably let sit at room temperature for 30 minutes before cooking. In a large, nonstick skillet, heat 1 tablespoon oil over medium-high heat until it is lightly smoking. Add as many pork belly slices to the pan as will fit in a single layer without crowding and cook, turning frequently, until caramelized on both sides and cooked through, 5 to 6 minutes. Transfer the pork to a medium bowl. Pour out the fat and rinse or wipe the pan clean. Repeat with the remaining pork belly, using 1 tablespoon oil to cook each batch. Set aside. (This pork is great on its own too.)

3   **Make the sauce:** In a medium bowl, whisk together all the ingredients, mixing well. Set aside.

4   **Prepare the rice cakes:** Preheat the oven to 400°F. Bring a medium saucepan filled with water to a boil. Add the rice cakes and boil for 5 minutes, then drain. The rice cakes must be used immediately after boiling. Dry the rice cakes very well on paper towels.

5   In a wok or large cast-iron skillet, heat the oil over high heat until it is lightly smoking. Add the rice cakes and let them sear until light golden brown on the underside. Then flip and let sear until the second side is lightly crisped, about 3 minutes. Add the fish cakes and cook, stirring occasionally, until heated through, about 2 minutes. Add the cabbage, onion, and carrot and cook, until softened, about 3 minutes.

SPICY PORK

1 small white onion, roughly chopped

3 garlic cloves

½-inch knob fresh ginger, peeled

1 tablespoon soy sauce

1 tablespoon water

¼ cup gochujang

2 tablespoons gochugaru

2 tablespoons Korean honey powder or sugar

2 tablespoons mirin

1 pound skinless pork belly, sliced ⅛ inch thick

Neutral cooking oil, for cooking

SAUCE

½ cup Anchovy Stock (page 47)

3 tablespoons gochujang

3 tablespoons rice syrup

1 tablespoon gochugaru

1 tablespoon soy sauce

1 tablespoon mirin

1 tablespoon Korean honey powder or sugar

2 garlic cloves, minced

RICE CAKES

3 cups cylinder-shaped rice cakes (garaeddeok), soaked in water for 30 minutes if frozen

2 tablespoons neutral cooking oil

¾ cup cut-up fish cakes, in 1-inch squares

½ cup thinly sliced green cabbage

½ cup thinly sliced onion

¼ cup peeled, thinly sliced carrot

6   Pour the reserved sauce over the mixture, turn down the heat to medium-high, and simmer until the sauce has thickened to a syrupy consistency, 1 to 2 minutes. Remove from the heat.

7   **Assemble the nachos:** If you have used a cast-iron or other ovenproof skillet to cook the rice cake mixture, you can leave the mixture in the pan. If not, transfer the rice cake mixture to a 10 x 10-inch square or round baking pan or dish. Layer the pork over the rice cake mixture, then top with both cheeses and the kimchi. Bake until the cheeses have melted and the sauce is bubbly, 7 to 10 minutes. Serve immediately.

NACHOS
1 cup shredded mozzarella
    cheese
1 cup shredded mild Cheddar
    cheese
1 cup drained, chopped cabbage
    kimchi

KIMCHI SALT POPCORN
김치 소금 팝콘

MAKES 10 CUPS

Fresh popcorn made on the stove top is really the best, and we've found it's the perfect vehicle for our kimchi salt, one of our favorite all-purpose seasonings. The salt will keep for months and marries the spice and kick of kimchi with the brightness of citric acid.

2 tablespoons neutral cooking oil

⅓ cup popcorn kernels

3 tablespoons unsalted butter

1 tablespoon kosher salt

1 tablespoon nutritional yeast

3 tablespoons shredded roasted nori seaweed (kim)

2 tablespoons Kimchi Salt (recipe follows)

1   In a 4-quart pot, heat the oil and three popcorn kernels over medium-high heat. When the kernels pop add the rest of the kernels, cover tightly, and shake the pot frequently to ensure the unpopped kernels fall to the bottom. The corn should begin popping soon after it is added to the pot, and it should pop constantly for 3 to 4 minutes. When the popping slows down (with 3 to 4 seconds between pops), it's time to turn off the heat and immediately transfer the popped corn to a waiting large bowl.

2   After dumping the popcorn into the bowl, wait for 1 minute for the pot to cool, then add the butter to the hot pot. Once it has melted and browned slightly, pour it over the popcorn and mix vigorously to distribute it evenly. You can return some of the popcorn to the pot and mix it around to soak up all the buttery goodness. Then add the kosher salt, nutritional yeast, seaweed, and kimchi salt and mix well to coat evenly. Eat right away.

Kimchi Salt: Korean Old Bay
김치 소금

MAKES ABOUT 3 CUPS

This is one of our favorite (and most popular) recipes from Koreatown, and we wanted to bring it back with a few tweaks. Deuki created this recipe with the intention of capturing the essence of kimchi in a powdered form.

1½ cups dried baby shrimp, or 1½ cups mushroom seasoning powder

½ cup garlic powder

½ cup onion powder

1 cup coarse gochugaru

1½ teaspoons ground coriander

1½ teaspoons citric acid powder

3 teaspoons ginger powder

1 cup kosher salt

1   Place the dried shrimp on a microwave-safe plate and cover with a paper towel. Nuke the shrimp in 30-second intervals, allowing the shrimp to air out for 30 seconds after each heating. Continue until the shrimp has turned slightly white, for 8 to 10 intervals. Once fully dried, allow the shrimp to cool for 15 minutes. (Don't be tempted to zap it all in one go—this will likely burn the shrimp.)

2   In a high-powered blender like a Vitamix Vita-Prep, combine the garlic powder, onion powder, gochugaru, coriander, citric acid, ginger powder, and dried shrimp. If you don't have a high-speed blender, pulverize the shrimp by themselves, in batches, in a coffee grinder and then mix all the powders together in a large bowl.

3   Thoroughly combine the mixed seasoning with the salt. The kimchi salt will keep in your pantry in an airtight container for several months.

A Los Angeles Korean Restaurant Crawl with Eater LA Editor Matthew Kang

We've been visiting Los Angeles Koreatown for well over a decade, and each time we return, there are at least half a dozen new places to drop in for a meal or a snack or a grilled lamb skewer. Matthew Kang, a Glendale native and the longtime editor of Eater LA, has been one of our favorite dining companions and sounding boards about what is happening within America's largest Korean American community. Kang has been writing about food since he was an undergraduate at USC, and before joining Eater as a full-time editor in 2014, he wrote a widely read blog on the side. He has run his own ice cream shop, filmed a popular Korean food YouTube series, and along the way he has been promoting Los Angeles Koreatown to anybody who would listen, including the late LA restaurant critic Jonathan Gold.

While visiting Los Angeles in the winter of 2023, we invited Kang to take us on a crawl of some of his favorite established and newer restaurants that are shaping today's Koreatown.

Kobawoo House

This is an absolutely legendary bossam spot that opened in 1983 and has been serving an iconic spread of spiced boiled pork and righteous haemul pajeon (seafood pancake) in a dining room that hasn't changed much since Ronald Reagan was in office. **Kang says:** "This is probably my favorite K-Town lunch special, with a sub-$20 bossam plate with banchan and all, but the eun daegu jorim (soy sauce–braised cod) and haemul pajeon are also spectacular. I filmed an episode of my YouTube show with my parents here, which I'm glad we did before my dad passed away. One day I'll show this to my son, Enzo, so he knows how much his harabeoji loved to eat." *698 South Vermont Avenue, #109, Los Angeles*

HanEuem

A recent opening at the time of our visit, the official name is HanEuem by Chef Kang (our Kang asked if Chef Kang was in the house to no avail). One of the specialties is a basket of eggy, silver-dollar-size jeon (modeum jeon) that are more common in Korea than in America. **Kang says:** "This feels like a hip Seoul restaurant placed into LA's Koreatown, and although [the food is] probably not as tasty as in the motherland, I appreciate the effort." *539 South Western Avenue, Los Angeles*

Yangmani

Lines and lines and lines. The lines are perpetual at this indoor-outdoor grill spot off Olympic Boulevard. So why are folks waiting in line? It's for the grilled guts: gopchang. It's for the beef intestine that is at once chewy, silky, and creamy. **Kang says:** "The cool, young Korean barbecue fans of LA would rather eat gopchang and daechang over expensive primal cuts." *2561 West Olympic Boulevard, Los Angeles*

Surawon Tofu House

There are a number of fresh tofu houses in Los Angeles, probably more in that city than anywhere outside of Seoul. But Surawon sets itself apart from the rest by making the tofu on-site. We rolled in just before the restaurant closed at 10:00 p.m., so we didn't get a chance to sit down. But Kang did spot LA chef Sang Yoon and chatted him up. **Kang says:** "It's one of the best all-around soon tofu spots in LA, and it took over what I think was a former Mexican restaurant. What's more LA than that?" *2833 West Olympic Boulevard, Los Angeles*

QUICK AIR FRYER NURUNGJI
햇반 누룽지

SERVES 1

Nurungji, or "scorched rice," is the highly prized layer of crisp, slightly charred rice found at the bottom of the pot. You can compare it to Spanish socarrat (the crusty bottom of paella). Nurungji is sometimes made into an end-of-meal tea, but the crisp, chewy rice also shines when dusted with sugar for a simple snack or ice cream topper. All you need to make it are instant rice, an air fryer (or a convection oven set to the same temperature and for the same timing), and about a half hour.

1 package (1 serving) instant rice (preferably Hetbahn brand)

2 tablespoons sugar

1 Cook the instant rice in a microwave according to the package instructions.

2 Lay a sheet of parchment paper on a work surface. Spread the rice in a thin layer on the parchment. To make spreading the sticky rice easier, use a spoon dipped in cold water.

3 Preheat the air fryer to 400°F. Place the rice on the parchment in the air fryer basket and cook for 20 minutes. Using a spatula, flip the rice over and toast on the second side to a delicious golden brown, 10 minutes longer.

4 Remove the rice from the air fryer and immediately sprinkle the sugar over the top. Eat immediately for the tastiest results, though it will keep for a couple of hours at room temperature.

TWO-MINUTE MANDU BAP
2분 만두밥

SERVES 1

This is the most dead-simple yet craveable recipe (more a serving recommendation or what we like to call a pro tip) you will find outside a bowl of Shin Ramyun — and it's for those times when you are sick of Shin Ramyun. Rice and dumplings go together like, well, rice and dumplings.

1 package (1 serving) instant rice (preferably Hetbahn brand)

6 to 8 frozen dumplings (such as Bibigo bulgogi mandu from Costco or your favorite)

1 tablespoon soy sauce

1 teaspoon sesame oil

1 package roasted nori seaweed (kim), shredded

1 Cook the instant rice in a microwave according to the package instructions.

2 In a small microwave-safe bowl, combine the dumplings with enough water to submerge them halfway, and microwave on high until hot, about 2 minutes. Drain.

3 Add the cooked rice to the bowl with the dumplings. Season with the soy sauce and sesame oil, sprinkle with the seaweed, and eat right away.

BANANA MILK CAKE
바나나맛 우유 케이크

MAKES ONE 6-INCH THREE-LAYER CAKE;
SERVES 4 TO 6

Elaine Lau is an accomplished pastry chef and creative force as well as Deuki's business partner at Neighborhood Bakeshop in San Francisco. One of our ideas was to develop a cake inspired by the flavors of the wildly popular convenience-store banana milks (banana mat uyu), which we always kept on hand in our Seoul apartment during visits. In America, flavored milks typically go in this order of popularity: chocolate way out in front, then strawberry (thanks to that weird Quik rabbit), and then maybe vanilla. In Korea, banana is, well, top banana. Lau came back with this stunning creation made with a layered vanilla chiffon cake, a banana cream filling, and a classic Swiss buttercream on top. Banana milk in cake form? Achieved with great results. Banana pastry often gets relegated to cream pudding status. This is the dessert to break it.

CHIFFON CAKE

3 eggs, whites and yolks separated, at room temperature

⅛ teaspoon cream of tartar

½ cup sugar

⅓ cup canola or other neutral oil

⅓ cup whole milk

2 teaspoons malted milk powder

½ teaspoon vanilla paste or pure vanilla extract

¾ cup cake flour, spooned and leveled

2 teaspoons baking powder

¼ teaspoon fine sea salt

1 **Make the cake:** Preheat the oven to 350°F. Lightly grease the bottom (avoiding the sides) of three 6-inch round cake pans with neutral oil or cooking spray, then line each pan bottom with a circle of parchment paper.

2 To make a meringue, in the bowl of a stand mixer fitted with the whip attachment, whisk the egg whites on medium-low speed until frothy, 1 to 2 minutes. Add the cream of tartar and whisk until blended. With the mixer still on medium-low speed, begin adding ¼ cup of the sugar, 1 teaspoon at a time, whisking until medium-soft peaks form, about 4 minutes. Increase the speed to medium and continue whisking until the peaks are nearly stiff, 6 to 8 minutes. Increase the speed to medium-high and whisk until stiff, glossy peaks form, 1 to 2 minutes. The meringue is ready when the whisk is lifted and turned upside down and the whites stand straight up without drooping.

3 In a large bowl, whisk together the egg yolks, oil, milk, milk powder, vanilla paste, and the remaining ¼ cup sugar, mixing well. Sift together the flour, baking powder, and salt into the yolk mixture. Gently whisk just until blended.

4 Fold the meringue into the yolk mixture in three equal batches, adding the next batch when about 80 percent of the previous batch is incorporated. Work as gently as possible so as not to deflate the mixture, especially near the end of folding. Fold in the final batch just until no white streaks remain.

5 Divide the batter among the three prepared cake pans. Stack two large sheet pans and place the cake pans on the stacked pans. Bake the cakes, rotating the sheet pans back to front halfway through baking, until browned on top and a toothpick inserted into the center comes out clean, 25 to 30 minutes.

6 Transfer the cake pans to wire racks and run a paring knife around the edge of each cake to release it from the pan sides. Let the cakes cool completely in the pans on the racks, about 1 hour. Turn the cooled cake layers out onto the racks, peel off the parchment, and turn upright. If desired, using a long serrated knife, trim the top of each cake layer to level it.

Recipe and ingredients continue

7   **Make the pastry cream:** While the cake layers are cooling, in a small saucepan, bring the milk to a simmer over medium heat, then remove from the heat.

8   While the milk is heating, in a medium bowl, mash the banana with a fork until smooth. Add the egg yolks, sugar, cornstarch, and salt and whisk until well mixed.

9   Add one-third of the hot milk to the yolk mixture while whisking vigorously to avoid cooking the yolks. Add the remaining hot milk in two equal batches, whisking vigorously during each addition. Strain the mixture through a fine-mesh sieve back into the saucepan.

10 Place the saucepan over medium-low heat and stir continuously with a silicone spatula. When the mixture starts to thicken, switch to a whisk. When bubbles start to appear on the surface, whisk continuously for 1 minute to cook out the starch. Remove from the heat. Whisk in the butter, a pat at a time, until melted, then whisk in the vanilla.

11 Transfer the pastry cream to a medium bowl and cover with a piece of plastic wrap, pressing it directly onto the surface (this helps keep a skin from forming). Refrigerate until well chilled before using.

12 **Make the buttercream:** Pour water to a depth of 1 to 1½ inches into a medium saucepan and bring to a simmer over medium heat. Combine the egg whites and sugar in a heatproof bowl and place the bowl on top of the saucepan. Make sure the bowl fits snugly in the rim without touching the water. Lower the heat to a bare simmer. Whisk the mixture continuously until hot to the touch and the sugar has dissolved, about 4 minutes.

13 Transfer the egg white mixture to the stand mixer fitted with the whip attachment and add the salt. Whisk on medium-high speed until stiff peaks form, about 15 minutes. Make sure the meringue has cooled to room temperature, then switch to the paddle attachment. On medium-high speed, add the butter, one or two pats at a time, beating until each addition is fully incorporated and the mixture is smooth and creamy before adding the next pat. When all the butter has been incorporated, beat in the vanilla, if using.

14 To assemble the cake, place a cake layer on a cake plate or stand. Top with half of the pastry cream and, using an offset spatula, spread it evenly to the edges. Repeat with a second cake layer and the remaining pastry cream. Top with the third cake layer. Rinse the offset spatula, then use it to frost the top and sides of the cake with the buttercream.

15 **Decorate the cake:** Slice the banana in half lengthwise and slice across into half-moon pieces. Place the pieces flat side up on a small sheet pan and sprinkle them with a thick, even layer of sugar. Using a kitchen torch, melt the sugar until it bubbles, melts, and then browns. Let cool completely and arrange decoratively on top of the cake.

PASTRY CREAM

1 cup whole milk

½ banana, peeled

2 egg yolks

¼ cup sugar

2 tablespoons plus 1 teaspoon cornstarch

⅛ teaspoon fine sea salt

7 tablespoons unsalted butter, cut into pats

¼ teaspoon vanilla paste or pure vanilla extract

BUTTERCREAM

3 egg whites

¾ cup sugar

Pinch of fine sea salt

1 cup unsalted butter, cut into pats, slightly cooler than room temperature

½ teaspoon pure vanilla extract (optional)

DECORATION

½ banana, peeled

Sugar, for sprinkling

GOCHUGARU CARAMEL CORN
고추가루 카라멜 팝콘

MAKES ABOUT 14 CUPS

In addition to being a killer pastry chef, Elaine Lau is a popcorn master. When we started collaborating on a Korean caramel corn, we wanted it to channel the spice and savoriness of kimchi but without the funky fermentation flavor. (You can look to our Kimchi Salt Popcorn on page 259 for more of that.) Here, gochugaru and a hint of soy sauce bring heat and rich umami to the basic Cracker Jack formula. We brought a few very large containers of this to a Super Bowl party, and it was gone before Rihanna took the stage.

3 tablespoons neutral cooking oil

½ cup popcorn kernels

2 tablespoons unsalted butter

4 teaspoons gochugaru

½ teaspoon soy sauce

½ cup granulated sugar

3 tablespoons brown rice syrup

2 tablespoons brown sugar

1¼ teaspoons kosher salt

¼ teaspoon baking soda

1   Preheat the oven to 300°F. Grease a large sheet pan with neutral oil or cooking spray.

2   In a large heavy-bottomed pot combine 1 tablespoon oil with 3 popcorn kernels. Cover and place over medium heat. When all 3 kernels have popped, add the remaining kernels. Put the lid back on the pot and shake to coat evenly.

3   When the kernels start to pop frequently, shake the pot often to prevent burning on the bottom. When the popping almost completely stops, uncover and remove from the heat. Sift through the popcorn to remove any kernels and spread out the popcorn on the prepared sheet pan. You should have about 14 cups.

4   In a small saucepan, combine the butter, gochugaru, soy sauce, and the remaining 2 tablespoons oil over medium heat. When the butter has melted, add the granulated sugar, rice syrup, brown sugar, and salt and stir to mix well. Bring to a full boil and continue cooking and stirring until the mixture registers 250°F on a candy thermometer, 1 to 2 minutes.

5   Add the baking soda to the caramel mixture and stir immediately until evenly combined. Pour the mixture evenly over the popcorn on the sheet pan and toss to coat evenly. It's fine if there are uneven patches of caramel.

6   Bake the coated popcorn, stirring every 5 minutes, until the caramel starts to thin out and coat the popcorn evenly, 15 to 20 minutes. Lower the oven temperature to 250°F and bake for 15 minutes longer to ensure the popcorn is nice and crispy.

7   Remove from the oven and let cool completely before serving. The caramel corn will keep in an airtight container at room temperature for up to a week.

DALGONA 3 WAYS
KOREAN HONEYCOMB CANDY (3 WAYS)
달고나

Dalgona is a honeycomb candy of lightly toasted sugar that is made by vigorously whisking baking soda into melted sugar so the sugar fizzes up and then solidifies, forming a crisp, airy treat. Dalgona was a popular Korean street snack in the 1970s and 1980s, and although it dipped in popularity for a bit, dalgona has in recent years had two big moments. First, whipped dalgona coffee (a direct inspiration from the candy, flavor-wise at least) exploded on TikTok. For it, you vigorously whip instant coffee with milk and sugar by hand or with an electric mixer to create a frothy, supersweet afternoon beverage. Second, dalgona candy played a role in a key plot point in the 2021 Netflix series *Squid Game*. (No spoilers about the plot, but it is worth saying that, as of this writing, *Squid Game* is the most-watched Netflix show *of all time*.) When we visited Korea to do research for this book, we spotted dalgona all over the place, and we wanted to create a recipe that expressed it in many forms. Here is a great recipe to make your own dalgona brick and three applications for it: a latte, a croissant, and a trail mix.

DALGONA BRICK
¼ cup water
1 cup sugar
2 teaspoons baking soda

1   Line the bottom of an 8-inch square baking pan with parchment paper. If you have a nonstick pan, you can skip the parchment. If you're making a dalgona croissant, you can skip the baking pan.

2   In a medium, heavy saucepan, combine the water and sugar over medium-high heat and heat, gently swirling the pan (don't stir) occasionally, until the mixture starts to turn a pale yellowish brown, 6 to 8 minutes. Do not let it get any darker or the candy will be bitter. The magical color is light amber.

3   When the correct color is achieved, remove from the heat immediately and add the baking soda. Working quickly, stir vigorously with a silicone spatula until fully incorporated and the mixture has grown in volume, about 10 seconds.

4   If using to make a latte or a trail mix, immediately transfer to the prepared pan. If using for a croissant, pour it over the baked croissants now. Let cool and harden for about 30 minutes. Follow the recipes below.

5   Crack the brick apart and enjoy. Or use to make a latte or trail mix (recipes follow). The candy will keep in an airtight container at room temperature for up to 1 week.

For a Latte
Break the dalgona brick into quarter-size pieces. For each serving, fill a tall glass with ice cubes and pour 1 cup whole milk over the ice. Add ¼ cup dalgona pieces (or less or more according to taste) to each glass. Pour an espresso shot (or an equal amount of double-strong French press coffee) over the dalgona, stir, and enjoy.

For Trail Mix
Break the dalgona brick apart. In a bowl, combine ½ cup salted cashews, ½ cup salted peanuts, ½ cup raisins, ½ cup chopped dried apricots (or other dried fruit), ½ cup nickel-size dalgona pieces, and ¼ cup flaked dried coconut. Mix well and enjoy.

For a Croissant
Use either home-baked or store-bought croissants (or home-baked or store-bought croissant dough). Make the dalgona brick mixture as directed, then pour about ¼ cup of the liquid over each croissant before it fully cools and hardens. The recipe makes enough for four or five croissants. Let cool and enjoy.

CANNED PEACHES AND RAISINS
복숭아와 건포도

SERVES 2 OR 3

YouTube is filled with Korean fruit factory videos. From pineapples and strawberries to lemons and grapefruits, creators like Yummyboy detail how fruit is juiced and canned on a large scale without fully losing its quality. Peaches are on another level, and many of the large food companies like Sempio and Penguin sell a product that is superior to what you will find in the United States – bright, slightly tart, and sweet. Adam Johnson's brilliant Pulitzer Prize–winning novel *The Orphan Master's Son* uses canned peaches as a critical plot device.

So here we are with canned peaches in a recipe. We had this at the end of a late-night meal in Seoul's Euljiro neighborhood, and it just really *worked*. Peaches act as a reset after a long session of overwhelmingly fishy and spicy flavors. And peaches and soju go together like peaches and . . . schnapps. This recipe is as simple as opening a can, but adding lemon amps up the tartness, which then accentuates the sweetness, and dried fruit adds a bit of chewy texture to go with the silky peaches. Crushed pistachios work well too. Have a can or two of Korean peaches on hand in case you get stuck on a dessert idea after a large feast.

One 15-ounce can peach slices (preferably a Korean brand)

Juice of ½ lemon

½ cup raisins, dried cranberries, or chopped dried stone fruit of choice

1   Drain the peaches of most of their juice, leaving a little (or more) according to your taste, and transfer to a small-to-medium bowl. Stir in the lemon juice.

2   Garnish with the raisins and serve.

FULLY LOADED SHIN RAMYUN
럭셔리 신라면

SERVES 2

According to Trigg Brown, chef and co-owner of Brooklyn's Taiwanese restaurant Win Son, "Shin Ramyun is the GOAT," he says of the universally loved Korean instant ramen brand known for its iconic heat and packaging. So why mess with perfection, as this recipe most skillfully does? "As amazing as this culinary touchstone is, it takes on further dimensions and personality as a vehicle for some chile oil and fermented bean curd," Brown says. So, yes, you can enjoy Shin Ramyun on its own, or you can throw in some eggs, Italian sausage, and (this is not a joke) Stacy's Fire Roasted Jalapeño Pita Chips. "Do this and you've got a real party," continues Brown. "Trust me and try it." We trusted, we tried, and here we are. It's an amazing take on a classic.

1 tablespoon neutral cooking oil

4 links hot Italian sausage casings removed

4 cups water

2 packages Shin Ramyun instant ramen

4 eggs

1 teaspoon jarred fermented bean curd with chile (dou fu ru)

One 3-ounce bag Stacy's Fire Roasted Jalapeño Pita Chips, crushed

½ bunch scallions, white and green parts, chopped

½ bunch cilantro, leaves and stems, chopped

1 pack snack-size sheets roasted nori seaweed (kim)

1 tablespoon LaoGanMa or Fly By Jing spicy chile crisp

1 Coat the bottom of a medium-to-large saucepan with the oil and heat over medium-high heat. When the pan is hot, add the sausage and cook, breaking it up with a fork, until browned and cooked through, 8 to 10 minutes. Transfer to a medium bowl and set aside.

2 In a medium saucepan, bring the water to a boil over high heat. While the water is heating, open the individual packets of dried vegetables and seasoning from the Shin Ramyun packages and reserve.

3 Have two individual serving bowls ready. Over a small bowl, crack an egg and pass it back and forth between the shells, allowing the white to drop into the small bowl and adding the yolk to a serving bowl. Repeat with the remaining eggs, dividing the yolks evenly between the two serving bowls. Reserve the egg whites.

4 When the water is boiling, add the ramen and the dried vegetables and seasoning. Cook the noodles, giving them a stir to make sure they're fully submerged so they cook evenly, according to the package instructions (about 3 minutes total). Once they are cooked, slowly pour in the egg whites while stirring constantly, followed by the fermented bean curd. Let cook for 1 minute longer.

5 Divide the noodles between the serving bowls, placing them on top of the egg yolks, then divide the soup (now thickened with egg whites and flecked with the hydrated vegetables) between the bowls. Top each bowl with the pita chips, scallions, cilantro, seaweed, cooked sausage, and chile crisp and serve immediately.

ICED YUJA CHA LEMONADE
냉유자 레몬에이드

SERVES 4 TO 6

This refreshing drink is made using yuja cheong, a honey citron tea concentrate. It combines tea made from the concentrate with lemonade for an extra citrusy and sweet lemon cooler. Serve with mint and lemon zest for a great mocktail, or add vodka or gin if you're going full steam. Replace the lemonade with sparkling water for a less sweet but still refreshing lemon soda.

Note: The base of a traditional Korean "tea," yuja cheong, a concentrate made from preserved yuzu (citron), honey, and sugar, is sold in jars at Korean markets and many Asian grocery stores. Follow the label directions to make the tea for this lemonade.

1 cup honey citron tea made from yuja cheong (see Note)
4 cups lemonade
2 cups water
Ice cubes, for serving
Fresh mint leaves, for garnish
Zest of ½ lemon, for garnish

1   In a blender, blitz the tea until smooth.

2   In a large pitcher, combine the tea, lemonade, and water and stir well.

3   Pour into ice-filled glasses, garnish with mint and lemon zest, and serve.

MISUGARU MILK
미숫가루 우유

SERVES 3 OR 4

Misugaru is a multigrain powder made up of a combination of roasted flours (typically a mixture of rice, wheat, and barley). While used in Korea for centuries as a cheap energy source, in modern times, it's been widely employed in Korean restaurants and home kitchens – in baking (cookies and breads), as a topping for bingsu (shaved ice), and mixed with liquids (especially milk) as a delicious drink. At Bodega Park in Los Angeles, chef-owner Eric Park utilizes misugaru in the most creative way: as a cold oat milk latte with a kiss of brown sugar. "Every Korean kid grew up drinking this. It's kind of like our version of Ovaltine," he says. This satisfying, refreshing drink, which can be served as a dessert at the end of a meal or at midday with a shot of espresso or instant coffee for a pick-me-up, is made with oat milk, brown sugar, and the multigrain mix. It pairs extremely well with the umami-rich cooking that may have preceded it.

2 cups high-quality oat milk

¼ cup misugaru powder

3 tablespoons brown sugar

Ice cubes, for serving

1 shot espresso or brewed instant coffee, cooled (optional)

1   In a blender, combine the oat milk, misugaru powder, and sugar and blend on low speed until well mixed. Using only low speed is important, as you want to incorporate all the ingredients but don't want the drink to be too frothy.

2   Pour into ice-filled glasses. Enjoy by itself or add an espresso shot for a delicious coffee drink.

JAE LEE IS A LOUD, PROUD, AND SOBER KOREAN CHEF

"I thought I had to act a certain way, being a pocha owner, which was totally backward." Jae Lee is sitting in an East Village café a few hours before service, sipping an iced coffee and talking about sobriety. His popular downtown bar and Korean-style comfort restaurant, Nowon, based on the tented Korean late-night restaurants called pojangmachas, is a few blocks to the south, and it's located in a pocket of NYC known for late-night partying. Lee, who is thirty-four and tattooed, grew up around New York City, mostly in Queens and on Long Island, living in Flushing, Floral Park, and Hicksville as an undocumented Korean immigrant. Initially, he loved to eat more than he liked to cook, and he never imagined a future career in food. But after a fluke job at a popular ramen shop, he was hooked and started to build a solid if not lucrative career working at places like the 1990s media power-lunch institution Michael's, Tabla under the late Floyd Cardoz, and eventually at Rice & Gold with Dale Talde. But at thirty, with his career at a crossroads, he decided to branch out on his own with Nowon, named after the northern Seoul neighborhood he grew up in.

The restaurant soon made a huge splash with Korean American stoner snacks like chopped cheese rice cakes, honey butter tots, and a double-stacked burger with kimchi mayo, bread-and-butter pickles, and American cheese. That burger is now called the Legendary Burger, and, no exaggeration, it sits on the podium of NYC burgers. Business at Nowon was steady for the first year until the pandemic happened, and then business became far from steady. Along the way as a chef, Lee had had a healthy relationship with alcohol—"healthy" meaning that he drank most days of the week.

"I always felt borderline unhealthy, and the pandemic made it way worse," he says of the days when he was working shorthanded and highly lubricated. "My only stress outlet was drinking. And I was the most stressed I had ever been in my life. I'd have a glass of wine or a beer. Then a friend would come, and we'd do a shot. The cycle would continue." One night, his staff ran service ten minutes later than the mandatory pandemic curfew imposed by the New York City government. Lee got upset and blew up, causing some employees to get emotional. He went home, filled with deep

shame. "Without my staff, I couldn't operate," he recalls of the night that changed his relationship to booze. "I was a slave to my emotions, and things needed to change." The next month, January 2021, he quit drinking. And he wanted to talk about it.

Korean food dances with alcohol to a never-ending song. We once spotted soju being slammed by a table of old men at an old-school juk spot near Seoul's city hall. It was just after 7:00 a.m. Soju and whiskey and wine and beer of all sizes are ordered with grilled kalbi, communal jeongol, and, naturally, late at night at the pocha-style restaurants that line the Koreatowns of America and around the world. We wanted to ask Lee about the complex relationship between alcohol and working as a Korean chef. "I prided myself on my ability to drink a lot as a Korean, and I was very good at holding my own," he says. "Being a chef, it's already part of the culture—on top of that, being Korean, it's double. So while owning a pocha-style restaurant was tough, I felt like I was giving up my identity." Yet Lee resolved to do it, and eventually, he found peace with the decision that he describes as perhaps not a lifelong choice, but something he is committed to now. "When you stop drinking, the number one outcome is that you face the reason you drink in the first place," he says. "I pride myself on being a sober Korean American chef. I feel very confident that way."

We get onto the topic of anju, the dishes that are almost canonically described as "drinking food" by Koreans and food writers. Lee pauses and smiles. "I was eating dinner with my dad last week, and I asked him, 'Is there Korean food that isn't anju?' And he was like, 'Everything is anju!'"

It's not far from our own experience. We've seen light tangs and salty dried fish called anju. Jeon is anju, and, of course, fried chicken slicked with sticky gochujang is anju.

And this is the biggest challenge when talking about sobriety and Korean food. Nobody wants to take the fun out of the Korean restaurant experience, especially Lee, who runs one of NYC's most fun and exciting places. And we are not ones to cast judgment. While we are not big drinkers, we think a round of soju is a fun time. But slipping out of the pattern a bit—rethinking Korean food's relationship with alcohol—is a topic we, and Lee, can't stop marinating on.

YUJA MINT SODA
유자 민트 소다

SERVES 1

This refreshing soda is a popular nonalcoholic item at Nowon in New York's East Village. Chef Jae Lee utilizes citrusy yuja cha (a "tea" made from sweetened yuja, a floral citrus fruit known in Japanese as yuzu) to build a syrup that will store for weeks in the fridge. This is perfect for a summer backyard banger where alcohol may flow (but not necessarily).

Ice cubes, for serving

1 ounce Yuja Mint Syrup (recipe follows)

1 ounce yuzu juice

About 6 ounces club soda

1 mint sprig, for garnish

Fill a glass with ice. Add the mint syrup and yuzu juice and top off with the club soda. Stir, garnish with the mint, and enjoy.

Yuja Mint Syrup
유자 민트 시럽

MAKES 1 CUP

1 In a small saucepan, combine all the ingredients over medium heat and bring to a boil, stirring often, until the sugar has dissolved, about 3 minutes. Remove from the heat and let cool to room temperature.

2 Transfer to a covered container and let sit at room temperature overnight. The next day, strain through a fine-mesh sieve before using. The syrup will keep in an airtight container in the refrigerator for up to several weeks.

1 cup firmly packed light brown sugar

2 tablespoons yuja cheong (honey citron tea concentrate)

1 cup water

6 mint sprigs

BOKBUNJAJU GINGER SOUR
KOREAN RASPBERRY WINE REFRESHER
복분자주

SERVES 1

Bokbunjaju is a popular fruit wine flavored with the juice of black raspberries. It's not very strong, and along with sipping it chilled, it's best when introduced into low-alcohol cocktails. This is one of our favorites – light and refreshing, and a perfect way to open your Korean dinner party or to sip on the patio while your kalbi cooks away. While reporting for this book, we had a spirited lunch in Gwangju with Rhea Lim, who runs the multigenerational and most prominent bokbunjaju producer in Korea. Lim represents the future of Korean spirits – a savvy marketer who's introducing this classic wine to a younger generation. While the traditional lunch was a highlight, we may have hit the black raspberry juice a little harder than we intended. Good times!

Here's a snappy citrus cocktail from prominent Seoul mixologist Yeongjun Jo. The bokbunjaju works really well with ginger and yuzu, but feel free to substitute lime juice for the latter. To make the ginger syrup, steep a 2-inch knob of peeled ginger in a 1:1 simple syrup. You can buy ginger syrup as well.

2 ounces bokbunjaju

1 ounce soju

½ ounce yuzu or fresh lime juice

½ ounce ginger syrup

1 egg white

Ice cubes, for chilling

1   In a cocktail shaker, combine the bokbunjaju, soju, yuzu juice, ginger syrup, and egg white. Cover and shake vigorously for 1 minute.

2   Add the ice to the shaker, cover, and shake again for 30 seconds. Strain into a cocktail glass and serve.

INGREDIENTS AND TOOLS:

STUFF TO KNOW, STUFF TO BUY

If you're a little new to cooking Korean food, the first thing you'll want to do is load up on the key ingredients. But here's some good news: Many Korean dishes can be made using products that are already common in Western home kitchens. These include garlic, ginger, scallions, soy sauce, sesame oil, tofu, and, of course, kimchi. And while specialty shopping is needed for some recipes, finding amazing Korean products has never been easier.

In this section, which is updated and revised from our first book, we want to familiarize you with some products you might not know as well and also touch on some common items that are used slightly differently in Korean kitchens. This is by no means an encyclopedia of Korean foods and tools, but it'll get you where you need to go with all the recipes in this book. And if you're stuck on something, hit us up on Instagram: @deukihong and @mattrodbard.

Ingredients and Tools

장 Korean Mother Sauces: Gochujang, Doenjang, and Ganjang

Much of Korean cooking is based around three essential, easy-to-find foundations called jangs, each one of which plays a role in creating the layers of flavor for which Korean cooking is famous. Here's our nickel jang tour:

고추장 Gochujang (Spicy Fermented Pepper Paste)

Identified by its bright red container, gochujang (pronounced go-choo-jahng) is a force in the Korean kitchen and is used in soups, stews, sauces, cookies (shout-out to Eric Kim), and barbecue marinades. It's savory, slightly funky (in the best way), and a little sweet, and it can be hotter than the chiles grown at Satan's CSA, so pay attention to the chile rating system on the packaging. The level two or three rating is typically our move.

Back in the day, gochujang was produced once a year, around the first day of spring. But with technological advancements and global demand, it's now pumped out of factories like ketchup. The process is relatively straightforward: meju, a cement-like block of dried and fermented soybeans, is mixed with red pepper flakes, barley, glutinous rice flour, and salted water, then left out in the sun to ferment and mellow for thirty to ninety days. In Korea, where virtually all jangs are produced, gochujang is aged in large earthenware pots. When used by itself, the flavor of gochujang can be a little too intense, so it's typically mixed with things like sesame oil, rice vinegar, garlic, ginger, and soy sauce.

된장 Doenjang (Fermented Bean Paste)

If gochujang is the fireworks at the Fourth of July celebration, doenjang (pronounced ten-jahng) is the music that plays along in the background. It's central to Korean cooking, deep and graceful but without the flash. To produce it, meju is rehydrated with salted water and left to ferment in the sun for many months. The liquid (ganjang, see page 289) is then separated to leave behind a thick, salty paste. This is doenjang, which is employed in many aspects of the Korean kitchen. The most widely known use is as the backbone of the barbecue condiment ssamjang (page 91).

Many cooks have suggested that Korean doenjang and Japanese miso can be substituted for each other in cooking, which is simply not accurate. Miso is typically sweeter and much milder, while the flavor of doenjang is intentionally in your face. Please, if you respect yourself, your fellow diners, and your Korean friends, do not use miso in any of the recipes in this book calling for doenjang. "You can call it 'miso' just like you call a girl a ho: that is, you can't," writes Los Angeles chef Roy Choi about doenjang in his memoir, *L.A. Son.*

간장 Ganjang (Soy Sauce)

As mentioned above, ganjang (pronounced gan-jahng) is the liquefied by-product from the production of doenjang—or, essentially, what everybody knows as soy sauce. In Korean cooking, two main types are available: regular and one used for soups. The regular variety is very similar to those found in China and Japan: salty, earthy, and packed with umami. The soup variety is unique to Korea. It is much lighter in color and sodium content and, as the name suggests, it is used in a variety of soup broths. It is also key when preparing namul (marinated vegetables). A good rule of thumb with soy sauce is to buy the low-sodium variety. Salt can always be added, but it can never be taken away.

Here are a few more things to keep on hand when cooking throughout this book. Sections on ingredients and gear can be super boring in cookbooks! We tried to make this one less so. Read it, and we promise you will learn something.

멸치젓 Anchovies (Myeolchi-jeot)

Some anchovies are fishy, others are mellow and briny, and all are sold in different sizes. They are used in many ways and act as a natural reminder of the ocean, which plays a major role in Korean cooking. Anchovy stock (page 47) is the base for many hot pots and requires a quality product. The good stuff, imported frozen from Busan, doesn't come cheap, running $10 to $15 per small box or bag. The best anchovies have healthy, shiny skin and are typically sold frozen; humidity is an anchovy's worst enemy, which is why you should keep these prized fish in the freezer.

고추 Chiles (Gochu)

In this book, we use both green and red fresh chiles, which are found at all Korean grocery stores. Korean green chiles are more vegetal than hot, closer to a bell pepper than a jalapeño. Thus, they are often added raw or lightly cooked to dishes as flavor enhancers. The long Korean red chile offers more heat. It's also used raw, but it is mostly dried and ground into gochugaru. If you need a Korean green chile substitute, try Anaheim chiles first and jalapeños next.

전기밥솥 Electric Rice Cooker

If you have the cupboard space and $30, an electric rice cooker is a very good investment. Nearly every Korean family has a rice cooker resting permanently (and prominently) in the kitchen. Most of the food cooked from this book is best enjoyed with a bowl of rice. While we offer a very good stove-top method (page 205), nothing beats the set-it-and-forget-it convenience of a rice cooker. And if you find yourself flush one afternoon, spend $200, and the thing will sing a K-pop song for you when the rice is ready.

액젓 Fish Sauce (Aekjeot)

We use fish sauce in a few dishes. It's not as much of a staple in Korean cooking as it is in Thai or Vietnamese cuisine. But for all our recipes, we highly recommend using Red Boat brand from Vietnam. The producers use only anchovies and salt, and they make their product the traditional way, with no fillers. You don't want to know what kind of filler is in some of the off-brand fish sauces you will find.

마늘 Garlic (Maneul)

For those who have never shopped at an H Mart or any other big Korean grocery store, a first trip to the produce section is a bit of a shocker. Good God, is there a ton of garlic there! Peeled and unpeeled. Pickled and pulverized. It makes sense, as Korea trails only China and India in annual garlic production, and once you've cooked anything at all in this book, you will realize that nearly every dish calls for a clove or twelve. Selecting good garlic is as easy as opening your eyes (make sure the bulb looks plump and healthy, not shriveled) and nose (if you're buying garlic already peeled, give it a whiff; the scent should be full and not faded). In a pinch, don't be afraid to buy minced garlic in a jar. If you cook your way through this book, you're going to use it.

주방 저울 Kitchen Scale

Five years ago, Matt bought a bright orange Escali Primo digital scale for $30, and he uses it every day. Let's start by saying that there is no downside to owning a digital scale. It's cheap, and it doesn't take up a lot of space. It's also essential for making great coffee (see page 65) and a great tool to have on hand when baking.

부침 가루 Jeon Mix (Buchim Garu)

Crisp, savory pancakes (jeon) are one of the most popular Korean foods, ordered at restaurants with particular glee. But here's a secret about those wonderful pancakes: they are almost always made from a mix, which you can find at all Korean grocery stores. Using a mix is a little funny given that so much Korean food is made from scratch, but this pancake mix saves time and is exactly what is used in restaurants: a blend of flour, baking powder, and cornstarch that helps with both texture and flavor. We use the packaged pancake mix in our jeon recipe (page 191), and we love the one that the fine folks at Queens in San Francisco sell (see page 294). Hit them up for a pouch.

김치 Kimchi

There's a widely accepted generalization that kimchi is exclusively the fermented cabbage product you found wedged atop a taco at your town's hip taqueria. While napa cabbage kimchi is one of the most popular types, other vegetables, such as daikon, cucumbers, and scallions, can also be "kimchi'd." Yes, we think of kimchi as more of a verb than a noun.

김치 냉장고 Kimchi Refrigerator

These small refrigerators (think dorm-room size) are widely sold in Korea and in appliance stores in the larger Koreatowns in the United States. If you are working on a crucial thirty-day kimchi fermentation, you don't necessarily want to be reminded of it every time you open your refrigerator door. If you plan on working your way through this book, have the space (like a garage or basement), and want to tell your friends that you're getting serious about Korean food, pick one up. It can hold your soju supply too.

막걸리 Makgeolli

Korea's oldest alcoholic beverage, makgeolli is a low-proof (around 6 percent alcohol by volume), unfiltered rice wine that was originally consumed by farmers at the end of long days. Good makgeolli is slightly effervescent and has a pleasant mouthfeel, similar to skim milk (it might sound a little weird to describe an alcoholic beverage this way, but you're going to have to trust us). Unfortunately, much of the makgeolli shipped to the United States is treated with preservatives to ensure it remains in good condition during the long journey.

미림 Mirin

A Japanese cooking wine, mirin is similar to sake, though with a very focused sweetness and a lower alcohol content. It's typically used in braises or marinades to tenderize meat, and the alcohol eventually cooks off. Alternatively, Koreans use mirin or mihyang, a light, alcohol-free cooking wine that is less sweet and intense than mirin.

깻잎 Perilla (Kkaennip)

Similar to Japanese shiso, perilla is used prominently in the Korean kitchen to wrap meat or to garnish soups and hot pots. Its flavor is vaguely mint-like, with hints of citrus. Perilla is found at any good Korean grocery store and most other Asian markets. In a pinch, you can substitute shiso, but do not substitute fresh mint.

무우 Radish (Mu)

What you will find in most Asian groceries is the almost ubiquitous daikon radish. Big, crisp, and juicy, the daikon is generally longer and thinner than the Korean ponytail or bachelor radish (chonggak), but it will work as a fine substitute for soups and stews. When making radish kimchi, however, it is best to seek out Korean radishes, which have a milder, sweeter flavor.

고춧가루 Red Chile Powder (Gochugaru)

Korean red chile powder is sold both coarsely ground and finely ground. The flavor is sweet and ever-so-slightly smoky, but the main function is to add heat. As you will find out, this ingredient can be H-O-T. We are going to say this just once: it's essential that you buy gochugaru, as cayenne pepper or red pepper flakes will not deliver the correct flavor. We've written all these recipes precisely for the flavor and heat level of gochugaru. Prices can range from a couple of dollars to nearly $20 for the Merck-grade artisanal stuff. And watch out for the gochugaru made from finely ground seeds, which is where the heart of the heat lives. Matt once bought a small bag at Tongin Market in Seoul and cooked with it back in New York. That was not pretty.

밥 Rice (Bap)

Rice is central to the Korean table, and it's served at basically every meal as either a side dish to accompany a sizzling sautéed plate or as the "glue" that binds together grilled meat and lettuce leaves. Rice can be served plain (ssalbap) or mixed together with barley (boribap) or millet (jobap). Koreans traditionally use short-grain rice varieties. Rice is so important in Korean culture that the popular greeting "Bap meogeosseoyo?" translates to "Have you eaten rice today?"

떡 Rice Cakes (Tteok)

Koreans love rice cakes, which are made by mixing glutinous rice flour with boiling water and salt, pounding the mixture into a dough, letting it set, and cutting it into a variety of shapes for different dishes. They can be slices, cylinders, or batons, and they have a unique texture—tougher and chewier than an Italian noodle—and are great at absorbing flavor. Rice cakes are always best when bought freshly made that day, which you can find at most Korean grocery stores. This is especially true of the cylinder-shaped variety used in the popular dish tteokbokki. You can also find rice cakes refrigerated and dried, both of which must be boiled before adding to a dish. Rice cakes are a fixture in the Korean kitchen and are eaten in quantities that are unrivaled by the Chinese and the Japanese, the world's two other great rice cake consumers.

식초 Rice Vinegar

This important acid is milder than Western vinegars. You can find it at any supermarket or health food store. And make sure not to substitute white or balsamic vinegar in any of these recipes, as they have very different flavors and acidity levels and won't translate. We like to use rice vinegar to cut through doenjang or gochujang in dipping sauces and meat marinades.

사케 Sake

Sake, the Japanese rice wine of sushi bar and "bomb" fame, is used in a few of our meat marinade recipes. The alcohol masks some of the more extreme "beefy" and "porky" elements that some Koreans don't necessarily like that much (while others adore them), but it also aids in tenderizing meat. When buying sake for cooking, the dry kind is best. And, of course, don't spend too much money on the bottle because it's going to go up in smoke anyway.

김 Seaweed (Kim)

The names can be a bit confusing, but in general, laver (English) = nori (Japanese) = kim (Korean), with nori the most widely recognized of the three in the United States. Koreans pride themselves on the seaweed farmed in the pristine waters off the country's southwest coast, and it comes in many forms. You are probably familiar with the small packages of roasted and seasoned dried nori seaweed squares sold in health food stores and Trader Joe's. That's one popular type of seaweed. We use it in a few noodle and rice bowl recipes, cut with scissors to act as a tasty garnish. Miyeok (also called wakame) is another type of seaweed, silky smooth when rehydrated in liquid and used in a birthday soup called miyeok-guk. Dashima, which is best known by its Japanese name, kombu, is used mostly in stocks. It is sold in fossilized sheets, and a little goes a long way. The takeaway from eating and cooking with seaweed? Do it. Its flavor is between that of a garden vegetable and a raw oyster. It's so unique that it's almost impossible not to love. Also, it's impossibly healthy too.

참기름 Sesame Oil (Chamgireum)

Some have called sesame oil the olive oil of Asia, which is on the right track. In Korea, high-quality sesame oil is valued so dearly that some cooks will source their own sesame seeds, roast them to their specification, and then take the seeds to a mill for grinding and pressing into oil. In Koreatowns in the United States, sesame oil dealers are neighborhood fixtures—and sometimes secretive. A *Los Angeles Times* writer was once chased out of a shop when she started to take a photo. The reason for all this effort is that once you've tasted a freshly pressed product drizzled over a bowl of rice or painted on a hunk of kalbi, there's no way in hell you are going back. The best bet is to buy a couple of bottles from an Asian grocery store and see which one you like (some are nuttier, while others tend to be sweeter, and calling one the best comes down to a matter of taste). Unless you are cooking at home a ton, it's best to buy sesame oil in small quantities and keep it refrigerated, as it can go rancid.

참깨 Sesame Seeds

Good (fresh) toasted sesame seeds should taste nutty. Bad (old, stale, turned) sesame seeds taste less nutty. You want nutty because nutty is the essence you are going for, not just texture or a pretty garnish for Instagram. If that container of sesame seeds has been sitting in the back of your pantry for five years, chances are they are in the less nutty category.

가위 Scissors

Just buy a pair of the Joyce Chen Original Unlimited Scissors, which are the best (ask any chef or food writer). They never get dull, they feel great in the hand, and they come in many cool colors. Ours are yellow. Scissors, used to trim vegetables, cut meat, slice noodles, and deal with tricky packaging, are your best friend in the Korean kitchen.

물엿 Syrups (Mulyeot)

The use of syrups in Korean cooking is widespread, and there are many different types. Mulyeot is clear and made from corn, while darker ssalyeot is made from rice—and both are available at any Korean grocery store. (Syrups made with barley and plums are sold there too.) Mulyeot and its many derivatives are lighter and slightly less processed than the corn syrup sold in the States. In a pinch, you can substitute honey, though you may want to cut back on the amount, as honey is sweeter and more floral.

소주 Soju

Soju is the national drink of Korea, where it is cheaper than bottled water. It tastes like a sweeter, milder vodka and can be mixed with basically anything. Generally speaking, it's a clear beverage distilled from rice, barley, wheat, or sweet potato. The alcohol content starts at about 15 percent and can go up to 45 percent in more premium bottles. In some places in the US soju is covered under a restaurant's license for beer and wine even though it is considerably more powerful than either one, creating a subgenre of soju-based cocktails (that, to be honest, often taste pretty terrible). Also, soju is often confused with shochu, a higher-proof and generally more refined distilled beverage commonly found in Japan.

뚝배기 Stone Bowls (Ttukbaegi)

Investing in a set of heatproof stone bowls is money well spent. They are great for both cooking directly on the stove top and serving up bubbling-hot stews (jjigae). Plus, they are easy to clean and they hold heat extremely well (almost too well, as those who have burned themselves an hour after their meal was served can attest). Koreans are famous for technological innovation (see that Samsung TV on your wall), but this is the ultimate lo-fi equipment.

두부 Tofu (Dubu)

The ubiquitous bean curd foodstuff you know as tofu is called dubu in Korea, but for the sake of clarity, we call it tofu in the recipes. There are many kinds of tofu available in both Asian markets and Western supermarkets, and in our recipes, we specify what type is needed. For soondubu jjigae, it's the extra-silken variety, while firmer tofu is used in fried and braised dishes. While we aren't loyal to a specific brand, it's always best to use the fresh stuff when possible. You can sometimes find freshly pressed tofu in Korean-owned markets or convenience stores. And if the Korean restaurant you are eating at makes its own, which is sometimes advertised proudly on signage, you are in for a treat.

Where to Find This Great Stuff!

As mentioned, there are numerous ingredients in this book that can be found at your regular grocery store. Many towns are home to both large Korean chains like H Mart and smaller, family-run grocery stores that carry the important jangs, frozen anchovies shipped straight from Busan, and dried seaweed. Matt's family lives in Kalamazoo, Michigan, which is located in the state's southwestern corner and has a modest-size Asian population. Yet it has a small Korean grocery store stocked with everything that's needed to cook from this book.

As a last resort, there are a number of online resources. Also, when you are bored at work, shopping online is sometimes unavoidable. Here are a few sites to get lost in.

Queens SF

Queens, located in San Francisco, is one of our favorite Korean markets anywhere, and it sells many of its products online, including a house-made gochugaru, sesame oil sourced from small producers in Korea, and an extremely good pancake mix that we use all the time.
queenssf.com

Kalustyan's

This New York City specialty store stocks more than four thousand spices, herbs, and teas, and it's a favorite of local chefs.
kalustyans.com

Crazy Korean Cooking

An extension of the smart K-food blog *Crazy Korean Cooking*, this Web-only store is a good place to find both necessary kitchen staples and equipment and a few quirky offerings—all with clearly written descriptions, which is a big plus.
shop.crazykoreancooking.com

ACKNOWLEDGMENTS AND THANK-YOUS

First up, **Deuki** and **Matt** would like to thank a few important people.

Nadia Cho, this all starts with you. Thank you for always being down to hang out in any kind of Korean restaurant, bar, café, pocha, or juk spot. Your generosity knows no limit. Amelia Ayrelan Iuvino, you are our copy rock. Thank you for the close reading, sound judgment, and enthusiasm for this book. We could not have done it without you. Young Sun Huh, thank you for the sharp recipe testing and helping us execute our sometimes vague and out-there vision.

Thank you to the literally hundreds of experts, chefs, journalists, and passionate food folks we spoke with to help us tell this sweeping story. Thank you to the restaurants that hosted us for meals and photo shoots, and thank you to the people of Korea for welcoming us with open arms and incredible kindness. While we cannot list all of those who helped us along the way, here are a few: Matthew Kang, Justine Lee, Vivienne Mo, Eric Kim, Tina Choi, Eunjo Park, Ji Hye Kim, Edward Lee, David Cho, Danny Lee, Yesoon Lee, Angel Barreto, Kate Telfeyan, Tory Miller, Jordan Michelman, Daniel Holzman, Lexie Park, Will Hu, Dale Talde, Sue Gee Kehn, Rani Cheema, Han Ly Hwang, Akira Akuto, Daniel Harthausen, Dennis Lee, Jason Stewart, Mingoo Kang, Peter Cho, Jen Chae, Danny Bowien, Ted and Yong Kim, Stella Pak, Lucas Sin, Susan Kim, Henry Park, BK Park, Nigel Price, Jason Ough, Jennie Kim, Clara and Eddo Lee, Elaine Lau, Yoon Sangah, Melissa Yoon, Jamie Oliver, Ruth Reichl, Robin Insley, and Will Matsuda.

And thank you to those who contributed recipes. We are deeply inspired by your creativity and love of cooking.

Deuki would like to thank

Jesus Christ, my Lord and Savior, who authors my life way more beautifully than I ever could.

To all the team members, partners, and investors of The Sunday Family. Your full trust in my leadership means everything to me.

My brothers, Alexander Chang, Charlie Hahn, and Peter Yoo. You guys are my rock. Let's celebrate. I'll see y'all at the Undefeated Lounge.

My mentors, new and old, I am nowhere without your guidance and wisdom in my life.

My mom and dad, who complained I used their made-up American name in the first book. So here it is: 홍성욱님 김미양님, 저는 두분의 아들이라서 너무 자랑스럽습니다. 사랑합니다.

My future wife and kids: we haven't met yet, but I promise I'm building something beautiful for us.

My brother Alex Lau, who is a savant behind the lens, but, more important, a nationally ranked powerlifter. That's it. I just want the world to know. Don't hate me, Lau.

My friend, mentor, and partner in crime, Matt Rodbard. This has been a ten-year (!!) journey, and there is no better human I would go on this journey with. Thank you for changing my life. So . . . when's book 3?

Matt would like to thank

This book would not have happened without the incredible support and creativity from the team at Clarkson Potter. Francis Lam continues to be the best in the business, and his support of this "not a sequel" from the jump was profound. Thank you, FL, you are always our guy. Major thanks to Susan Roxborough and Darian Keels for the sharp edits and deep creativity when hammering out the final innings of the manuscript. Thanks to our amazing designer, Robert Diaz, for helping execute our big design ideas, and to our crack marketing and PR team, specifically David Hawk, Stephanie Davis, and Natalie Yera. Thank you to our production editor, Terry Deal, your enthusiasm is so appreciated. Thanks to Sharon Silva for putting the book through a very fine strainer.

And a huge thanks to my longtime colleagues at the Crown Publishing Group and those around the building at Penguin Random House: David Drake, Aaron Wehner, Jill Flaxman, Windy Dorresteyn, Allison Renzulli, Raquel Pelzel, Jenn Sit, Pat Stango, and Shalea Harris. And to all of my colleagues and collaborators at *TASTE,* especially Anna Hezel and Aliza Abarbanel. You are the absolute best.

Thank you to our longtime agent and friend, Angela Miller, who has remained a measured and always enthusiastic person in our corner. Thanks to Neil Russo for always knowing what to say and for always being game to order more bokkeumbap. Thanks to Apple Computer, Google Docs, Adobe, Zoom, and Slack.

Thank you to my family in Michigan, New Jersey, and Virginia. Thank you to Cheryl, who eats more kimchi before nine a.m. than anyone I know.

Alex: You are our bro and one of the coolest, kindest, naturally chill, and incredibly talented photographers around. Look at these photos! Thank you, Alex.

Deuki: Tamar still calls you baby Deuki, but you are most certainly not a kid anymore. I've watched you grow in so many ways. Your golf game, it's nice. Brother, you are an inspiration to all who are fortunate to land in your world, be it while running a kitchen or speaking about important issues into a microphone. I'm proud of you and will forever be your collaborator and friend.

And Tamar, thank you for the bottomless fountain drink of love and support for not just this book but for all the editorial work that gives me so much joy. I will always be the Dr Pepper next to your Coke Cherry Zero.

INDEX

바다향기로 계단

SOKCHO

천천히

Published in the United States by
Clarkson Potter/Publishers, an
imprint of the Crown Publishing
Group, a division of Penguin
Random House LLC, New York.
ClarksonPotter.com

CLARKSON POTTER is
a trademark and POTTER
with colophon is a registered
trademark of Penguin Random
House LLC.

Library of Congress Cataloging-
in-Publication Data is on file with
the publisher.

ISBN 978-0-593-23594-2
Ebook ISBN 978-0-593-23595-9

Printed in China

Editors: Francis Lam
and Susan Roxborough
Editorial assistant: Darian Keels
Designer: Robert Diaz
Production editor: Terry Deal
Production manager: Kim Tyner
Compositors: Merri Ann Morrell
and Hannah Hunt
Recipe tester: Young Sun Huh
Copyeditors: Amelia Ayrelan
Iuvino and Sharon Silva
Proofreaders: Lorie Young and
Marlene Tungseth
Indexer: Barbara Mortenson
Publicists: David Hawk and
Natalie Yera
Marketer: Stephanie Davis

10 9 8 7 6 5 4 3 2 1

First Edition

Clarkson Potter/Publishers
New York
clarksonpotter.com

Cover design: Robert Diaz
Cover photographs: Alex Lau